From Your Friends at The MAILBOX®

Light & Sound

Grades 4–6

INVESTIGATING SCIENCE

Project Manager:
Cindy Mondello

Writers:
Marcia Barton, Ann Blackwood, Gail Peckum
Stephanie Willett-Smith

Editors:
Cayce Guiliano, Peggy W. Hambright, Deborah T. Kalwat
Scott Lyons, Jennifer Munnerlyn

Art Coordinator:
Clevell Harris

Artists:
Theresa Lewis Goode, Nick Greenwood, Clevell Harris,
Rob Mayworth, Greg D. Rieves

Cover Artists:
Nick Greenwood and Kimberly Richard

www.themailbox.com

©2000 by THE EDUCATION CENTER, INC.
All rights reserved.
ISBN #1-56234-437-4

Manufactured in the United States

10 9 8 7 6 5 4 3 2 1

Table of Contents

About This Book

Welcome to *Investigating Science—Light & Sound*! This book is one of eight must-have resource books that support the National Science Education Standards and are designed to supplement and enhance your existing science curriculum. Packed with practical cross-curricular ideas and thought-provoking reproducibles, these all-new, content-specific resource books provide intermediate teachers with a collection of innovative and fun activities for teaching thematic science units.

Included in this book:

Investigating Science—Light & Sound contains five cross-curricular thematic units, each containing

- Background information for the teacher
- Easy-to-implement instructions for science experiments and projects
- Student-centered activities and reproducibles
- Literature links

Cross-curricular thematic units found in this book:

- *Reflection*
- *Refraction*
- *Color*
- *Sound*
- *Hearing and the Ear*

Other books in the intermediate Investigating Science series:

- *Investigating Science—Space*
- *Investigating Science—Weather & Climate*
- *Investigating Science—Plants*
- *Investigating Science—The Earth*
- *Investigating Science—The Human Body*
- *Investigating Science—Animals*
- *Investigating Science—Energy, Magnetism, & Machines*

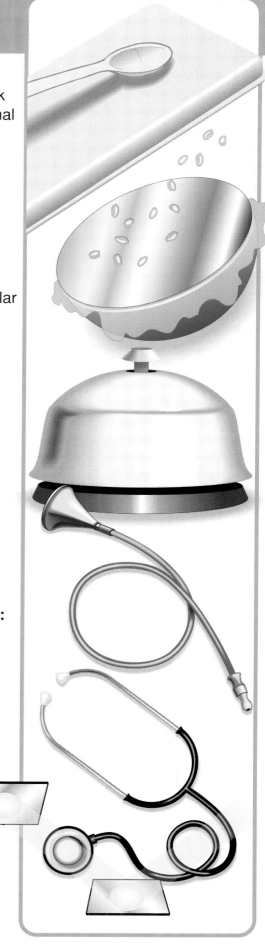

Reflection

Help students reflect on ways to make light bounce with this illuminating collection of activities, experiments, and reproducibles.

That's the Way the Light Bounces
(Demonstration)

What do rubber balls and light beams have in common? Help students find out by performing this simple demonstration. Have a student go to the front of the class, hold a rubber ball waist high, and then drop it. Ask the class to describe what the ball does *(bounces back up to the student's hand)*. Have another student stand several feet from Student A. Direct Student A to bounce the ball at an angle to Student B. Ask the class to describe the ball's bounce *(bounces at an angle from Student A to Student B)*. Instruct Students A and B to bounce the ball between them at different angles. Tell the class that the way the ball bounces (in a straight line) is how light bounces, or *reflects,* from mirrors and other flat, shiny surfaces.

Next, copy the drawing below onto the board. Explain that the *angle of incidence* (the angle at which light from an object hits the mirror) equals the *angle of reflection* (the angle at which light rays from the object are reflected). Point out that this is how people are able to see images in a mirror even when they cannot see themselves in it— because they are standing in the angle of reflection. Have each child try this at home using a large mirror and report her findings to the class. To help students discover that light not only travels in straight lines but around corners, too, have them complete the periscope project on page 10 as directed.

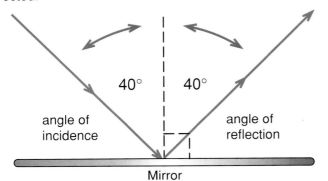

angle of incidence   40° | 40°   angle of reflection

Mirror

Background for the Teacher

- *Light* is a form of energy called *radiant energy* that travels freely through space.
- *Visible light,* referred to simply as *light,* is the only type of radiant energy that's visible.
- In addition to visible light, infrared rays, radio waves, ultraviolet rays, and X rays are all kinds of radiant energy.
- Light is produced by atoms that have gained energy after being struck by other particles or that have absorbed light from another source.
- A *mirror* is a flat, smooth surface made by putting a thin layer of silver or aluminum onto a sheet of high-quality glass.
- Mirrors *reflect* (bounce back) most of the light that strikes them.
- The image seen in a *plane* mirror (one with a flat surface) is the same size as the reflected object, but reversed from left to right.
- *Concave* mirrors curve inward and make images appear larger.
- *Convex* mirrors curve outward and make images appear smaller.

An Enlightening Literature List

Experiments With Light and Mirrors (Getting Started in Science series) by Robert Gardner (Enslow Publishers, Inc.; 1995)

Light and Sight (Science Factory series) by Jon Richards (Copper Beech Books, 1999)

Light FUNdamentals: FUNtastic Science Activities for Kids by Robert W. Wood (McGraw-Hill, 1996)

Mirrors: Finding Out About the Properties of Light by Bernie Zubrowski (William Morrow and Company, Inc.; 1992)

Bouncing Off the Wall
(Drawing and Measuring Angles)

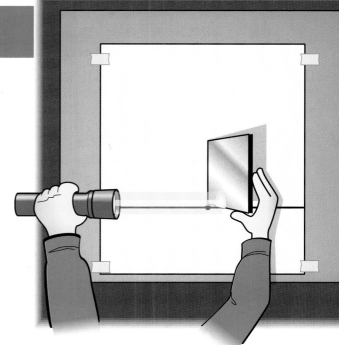

Observe light beams bouncing off the wall with this attention-grabbing activity. Gather a flashlight and a small rectangular mirror for each student (or group of students). Number five sheets of dark-colored construction paper; then mount them in order and level with students' desktops on a classroom wall. Have each child sit at her desk facing the papers. Give each student a mirror, a flashlight, a plain sheet of paper, four pieces of tape, a ruler, and a protractor. Direct her to tape her paper to the desktop and to complete each step below as you model it for the class. When students have finished measuring the angles, ask why the measurements varied for each target *(students sat in different locations, beams of light hit different spots on the paper targets, etc.)*. For more angle-measuring practice, give each student a copy of page 11 to complete as directed.

Steps:
1. Use the ruler to draw a horizontal line across the paper.
2. Make a dot (the vertex of the angles to be drawn) anywhere along the line.
3. Place the flashlight on the desktop, aligning it with the line on the left side of the paper.
4. Place the left corner of the mirror on the dot and turn the flashlight on. Darken the room, if necessary. Pivot the mirror (not the flashlight or paper) on the dot until the reflected light hits Target 1. Keep the mirror in this position.
5. Draw a ray by tracing a line on the paper along the straight edge of the mirror. Label the resulting angle "Angle 1."
6. Continue in this manner, pivoting the mirror to hit each target, in turn, and then drawing each successive angle and labeling it "Angle 2," "Angle 3," etc.
7. Use the protractor to measure each angle in degrees. Record each measurement next to the corresponding angle.

Reflector Race
(Following Directions, Making Observations)

Let students experience the amazing characteristics of reflected light by having them make light beams zigzag through the classroom. Give each child a mirror. Next, have students hold the mirrors waist high and stand facing one another in two parallel lines about three feet apart. Darken the room completely and shine a laser pointer (or flashlight) at the mirror of the first child in line. Direct that child to use his mirror to reflect the light to the mirror—*not the eyes*—of the child across from him. Have that child reflect the light to the child across from him, and so on, until the zigzagging light beam reaches the last child in line. If desired, allow students to practice until they can zigzag the light with more speed. Then divide students into teams that race to be first at getting the light beam to the end of the line. As a final challenge, have teams try to reflect the light in zigzagging patterns of alternating short and long beams.

Making Money Grow...With Mirrors!
(Student Investigation)

Can mirrors really make money grow? In a manner of speaking, yes! Use this simple investigation to prove it. Tape two same-sized rectangular mirrors together along one side (faces together) to make a hinge that opens and closes easily. Place the mirrors and a dime at a center. Direct students using the center to open the mirrors into a straight line behind the dime and to slowly bring the mirrors' faces together to see the number of images grow from 2 to 14 dimes. *(When positioned at different angles, each mirror reflects an image that can be reflected again. The closer the two mirrors become, the more images they can reflect.)* Have students repeat the investigation using different-sized objects, such as a paper clip or a pencil holder, to see if the number of reflected images varies *(the wider the object, the fewer the images that can be reflected).* Or have each student create a "hall of mirrors" by separating the mirrors and propping each one against a stack of books so that they are parallel to each other. Then have her place a dime between the mirrors, place her eye close to the edge of one mirror, and look sideways into the other mirror to view multiple reflections of the dime.

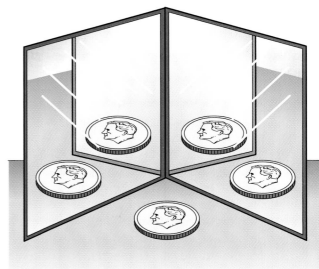

Colorful Kaleidoscopes
(Following Directions, Writing Descriptions)

Let students delve deeper into the world of mirrored illusions by having them create their own simple kaleidoscopes. First, allow students to look into a real kaleidoscope and hypothesize about how such toys are made. Next, give each student three same-sized rectangular mirrors to tape together into a triangular tube as shown. Have the student place the triangular tube upright on a colorful magazine picture and trace around the tube. Direct him to cut out the tracing, leaving a half-inch border, and then tape it over one end of the triangular tube with the picture facing inward. To use the kaleidoscope, have the student look in the open end of the tube while rotating it in his hand. Allow students to trade toys and observe the variety of patterns that can be created. Follow up by asking each child to write a vivid description of the colorful images that can be viewed by looking inside his kaleidoscope.

Amazing Artists
(Following Directions)

Magically transform students into talented artists with a little help from reflected light! Gather as many flat, rectangular pieces of glass from picture frames as possible. For safety, cover the edges of each piece with masking tape. Divide students into groups, one group for each piece of glass. Give each group a piece of glass, magazines, and a flashlight. Give each student scissors and one sheet of drawing paper. Have each child cut out an interesting magazine picture, one that contains no writing and is smaller than her group's piece of glass. Direct one child to hold the glass upright on a desktop while another places her magazine picture faceup on one side of the glass and her sheet of drawing paper on the other. Instruct a third child to turn on the flashlight and place it at the top of the picture so that the light shines on the picture, not directly on the glass. Darken the room; then have the student trace her picture's reflection onto the drawing paper. The result? An instant masterpiece, ready to be colored!

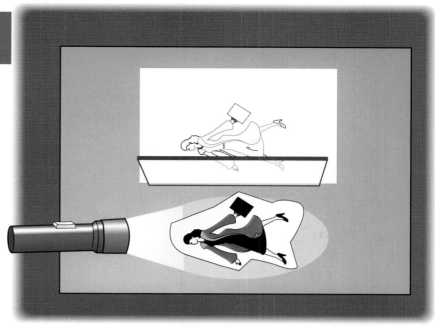

Flip-Flopped Images
(Demonstration, Making Observations)

What can change shape and flip reversed images rightside up in a snap? The human eye and its partner, the brain! Allow students to observe this scientific fact by conducting the demonstration below. Afterward, copy the illustration of the eye onto the board, using it to explain to students exactly how the eye and brain perform this feat. Point out that the convex lens in the eye bends incoming light and adjusts automatically to become rounder and thicker or flatter to help us view close or distant objects. Also point out that the lens focuses the image upside down on the retina at the back of the eye and that nerve signals sent to the brain flip the image rightside up. Continue the flip-flopped fun—this time helping students understand how mirrors reverse images—by giving each student a copy of page 12 to complete as directed.

Materials: plain white paper, tape, candleholder, candle, matches, magnifying glass, unshaded electric lamp with bulb

Steps:
1. Tape the paper to a wall at desktop height.
2. Place the candleholder and candle on the desktop about one foot away from the paper. Light the candle. Then darken the room.
3. Holding the magnifying glass approximately halfway between the lighted candle and the paper, have one student at a time stand a safe distance away from the candle and look through the magnifying glass to see an image of the candle's flame on the paper. If necessary, move the magnifying glass back and forth to get a clearer image. Have each student describe what she sees. *(The flame's image on the paper is upside down.)*
4. Repeat Steps 2 and 3 using the unshaded lamp in place of the candle. *(The lightbulb's image on the paper is upside down.)* Ask students what the lens in the magnifying glass and the white paper represent. *(The lens represents the eye's lens and the white paper represents the retina.)*

opaque

translucent

transparent

Seeing...Clearly, Fuzzily, or Not At All
(Classifying Objects)

Make the meanings of the terms *transparent, translucent,* and *opaque* crystal clear to students with this hands-on classification activity. First, explain the following terms shown in the box below. Next, divide students into groups of four. Give each group a flashlight and a box containing an assortment of transparent, translucent, and opaque objects, such as writing paper, newspaper, plastic wrap, a tin can, plain glass edged with masking tape, frosted glass edged with masking tape, waxed paper, a magnifying glass, sunglasses, a latex glove, construction paper, tissue paper, aluminum foil, a white plastic lid, a leaf, etc. Have each student hold each item up to the flashlight, observe the amount of light that passes through it, and then list it in a chart accordingly as shown. After students share their results with the class, challenge them to think of three more objects that could be added to each category.

- *Transparent*—a material that does not mix light rays and allows a person to see through it clearly
- *Translucent*—a material that mixes light rays and allows a person to see through it, but not clearly
- *Opaque*—a material that blocks all light rays, preventing a person from seeing through it at all

Transparent (can see through clearly)	Translucent (can see through, but not clearly)	Opaque (cannot see through at all)
glass plastic wrap	waxed paper latex glove	aluminum foil white plastic lid

Mirror, Mirror, How Big Should You Be?
(Linear Measurement, Data Interpretation)

How large must a mirror be to reflect an object's entire height? Challenge students to find out by conducting this interesting investigation. Divide students into groups of four. Give each group the materials listed below. Instruct one member of the group to copy the chart. Then guide the groups through the steps to collect the data. After all the data has been collected, ask students to look for a relationship between the height of each picture and the distance between the lines. *(The distance between the lines on the mirror is about half the height of the actual picture.)* Help students conclude that a mirror should be about half the object's size to reflect its entire height. Challenge students to test this rule by standing in front of a door (or wall) mirror at home or at a department store.

Materials: magazine, scissors, hole puncher, wipe-off marker, ruler, paper towel, sheet of loose-leaf paper, handheld mirror

Steps:
1. Cut out four full-length pictures of people of different heights.
2. Label the cutouts "A," "B," "C," and "D." Punch a hole in the middle of each cutout's head.
3. Have one group member hold up the mirror, while another holds Picture A a short distance away.
4. Direct the student holding the picture to look through its punched hole and back away from the mirror one step at a time, stopping in place when he sees both the top and bottom of the cutout's reflection. Have him use the marker to make two horizontal lines on the mirror to show the location of the top and bottom of the picture.
5. Have another group member measure both the height of the picture and the distance between the lines on the mirror, record the measurements in the chart, and then use a wet paper towel to clean the mirror.
6. Have group members switch roles and repeat Steps 3–5 for Pictures B, C, and D.

Picture	Picture Height	Distance Between Lines on Mirror
A	4$\frac{1}{2}$"	2$\frac{1}{4}$"
B	3$\frac{1}{2}$"	1$\frac{3}{4}$"
C	6$\frac{3}{4}$"	3$\frac{3}{8}$"
D	9"	4$\frac{1}{2}$"

Crazy Reflections
(Classifying Objects)

Does a curved surface reflect light in the same way as a plane surface? Challenge students to find out with this hands-on activity. Provide small groups of students with several reflective test items that are not flat planes, such as a spoon, glass Christmas tree ball, pan lid, bike reflector, shiny doorknob, makeup mirror, sunglasses, etc. Appoint a recorder in each group to copy the chart below onto a sheet of paper. Then have different members of each group test the items one at a time, first holding the item close to the face and then at arm's length and record the results. After all the items have been tested, discuss with students the differences between *convex* and *concave* mirrors. Point out that a convex mirror curves outward and makes objects appear smaller and farther away and that a concave mirror curves inward and makes objects appear larger and closer. Conclude by having groups classify each item as convex or concave and then share their answers with the class.

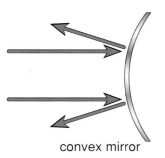

convex mirror

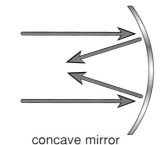

concave mirror

Test Item	Description of Reflected Image	Classification
Inside of spoon	large, upside down	concave
Outside of spoon	small	convex
Shiny doorknob	small	convex
Makeup mirror	large	concave

Temperature-Raising Reflectors
(Experiment)

What effect can concave mirrors have on raising water temperature? That's what students will test in the following experiment. After students conduct the experiment, discuss the results together, explaining that solar ovens used by campers work in the same way. Have students suggest foods that could be cooked using this method. Then, if desired, bring in a solar oven and cook some of the foods to demonstrate!

Materials: two 12" x 18" sheets of poster board, one covered with aluminum foil; three 9-oz. plastic cups, each filled with tap water; 3 thermometers; stacks of books; 1 watch

Steps:
1. Measure the water temperature in each cup and record it.
2. Take the cups of water outside and place them on a sunny sidewalk.
3. Curve the foil-covered paper halfway around one cup to make it face the sun. Stack books behind the paper to hold it in place.
4. Curve the plain paper behind the second cup in the same way.
5. Make sure the third cup is in a place where it will not be affected by either sheet of paper.
6. Put a thermometer in each cup. After 30 minutes, measure and record the temperatures. Discuss the findings. *(The water temperature of each cup is different. The cup partly surrounded by the foil-covered paper has the highest temperature because the shiny concave surface focuses the incoming light and heat onto the cup and its contents. The cup with nothing surrounding it has the coolest temperature.)*

Periscope Peeks

Pretend you've just been hired by the famous Peterson Peabody, Private Eye. How can you become his most valuable helper? Would a periscope help? No one would be safe from your spying if you could see over tall walls! Follow the directions below, and you can be spying in a snap!

Materials:
half-gallon milk or juice carton (the
    cardboard kind)
2 small rectangular mirrors
scissors
tape
ruler

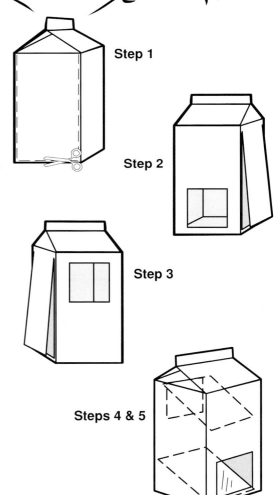

Steps:

1. With your teacher's help, cut along one side panel of the carton to create a flap.

2. In the side to the left of the flap, cut an opening that is two inches square and one inch from the *bottom* edge.

3. In the side to the right of the flap, cut an opening that is also two inches square but one inch from the *top* edge.

4. Lift the flap and tape one mirror faceup at a 45° angle to the side opposite the lower opening.

5. Tape the remaining mirror facedown at a 45° angle just above the upper opening and parallel to the bottom mirror.

6. Close the flap. Hold the periscope so that its top opening is above the top edge of a tall object, such as a bookcase, and look into the bottom opening. You should be able to see what's on the other side. If not, adjust the angle of the mirrors slightly and try again. Happy spying!

Step 1

Step 2

Step 3

Steps 4 & 5

Bonus Box: On the back of this page, describe three occasions when it would be helpful to have a periscope to help you see over tall objects.

What Are They Looking At?

Each child below sees a different object in the mirror. Mirrors reflect light. The angle at which light strikes a mirror is called the *angle of incidence.* The angle at which light reflects from the mirror is called the *angle of reflection.* Follow the directions below to match each child to the object he or she sees. If you match them correctly, you'll learn another name for a flat mirror!

Steps:

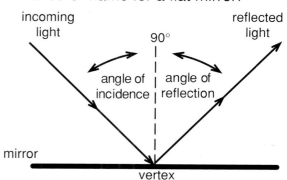

1. Place the protractor on the dotted line below. Align the center of the protractor with the *vertex,* the point where all the angles hit the mirror. Measure the angle between the cat and the dotted line. Record the measurement in degrees in the blank next to the cat.
2. Keep the protractor in place and measure and record the angles of the cake, apple, banana, and dog.
3. Using the straight edge of the protractor, draw line segments connecting the vertex on the mirror with the nose of each child.
4. Repeat Step 1, measuring the angle between the dotted line and each child. Record each measurement in degrees in the top blank next to each child.
5. Identify the object each child is looking at by matching the number of degrees. Then write the name of the object in the second blank.

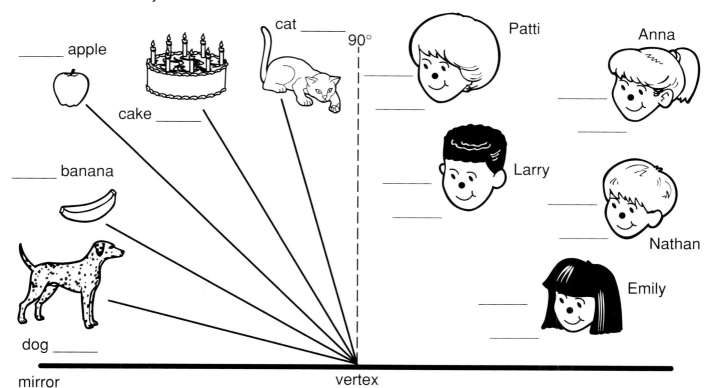

Now learn another name for a flat mirror by writing the first letter of each child's name in the following blanks in order from least to greatest number of degrees. ____ ____ ____ ____ ____

Bonus Box: Add another child and an object he or she is looking at to the diagram above. Position the drawings so their angles of incidence and reflection are equal to 80°.

©2000 The Education Center, Inc. • *Investigating Science* • Light & Sound • TEC1737 • Key p. 48

Note to the teacher: Use after "Bouncing Off the Wall" on page 5. Each child will need a protractor to complete this activity.   11

Flip-Flopped Messages

Does the writing on the mirrors below look strange? That's because images in mirrors are reversed. Find out what each flip-flopped message says by placing a mirror on the corresponding dotted line. Record each decoded message on the back of this page. Then do what each message directs you to do!

1. Draw a smiley face at the top of this paper.

2. Write your first, middle, and last name in the bottom left corner.

3. Draw a sun in the upper right corner.

4. Write a sentence using the word "reflection" on the back of this page.

5. Which travels faster, light or sound? Write the answer five times in the lower right corner.

6. List your three favorite foods on the other side.

7. Copy the statement "The angle of incidence equals the angle of reflection" anywhere on this paper.

8. Write the name of an object that is good at reflecting light in the upper left corner.

Bonus Box: Leonardo da Vinci, an Italian scientist and artist, used mirror writing to record many of his notes. Write a message on a sheet of paper. Next, place a mirror on the paper above the message and copy its reflected words onto another sheet of paper. Then challenge a classmate to use a mirror to decode the message.

The Camera's Cousin

Long before cameras and photographs were invented, people viewed images through a *camera obscura,* which is Latin for "darkened room." The first camera obscura (from almost a thousand years ago) was based on the discovery that by passing sunlight through a small hole in one wall of a darkened room, an image of the sun was formed on the opposite wall. By the 1660s, portable camera obscuras were available. People used them to view the sun and to look at streets and landscapes. With your partner, follow the steps below to make a camera obscura.

Materials: empty Pringles® can, 9" x 11" piece of black construction paper, pushpin, masking tape, pencil, clear tape, ruler, scissors, utility knife (to be used by your teacher)

Steps:

1. Remove the lid from the can.
2. Use your pencil to trace a line around the can about 2¹/₂ inches up from its bottom edge.
3. Have your teacher cut along the pencil line with a utility knife to divide the can into two pieces.
4. Use masking tape to tape the lid atop the open end of the smaller piece. Use the pushpin to make a hole in the center of the plastic lid. Place the larger piece atop the smaller one.
5. Tape the two pieces together using masking tape.
6. Wrap black construction paper around the tube and trim it to size. Tape the construction paper securely in place using clear tape.
7. With your teacher's help, use the pushpin to punch a small hole in the center of the metal end of the can.
8. Take the model outside on a sunny day and hold the open end of the tube up to your eye. Wrap your hands around the tube near your eye as you point the tube at a stationary object three to five feet in front of you.
9. With your partner, take turns looking at the object using the model.
10. On another sheet of paper, describe what you see.

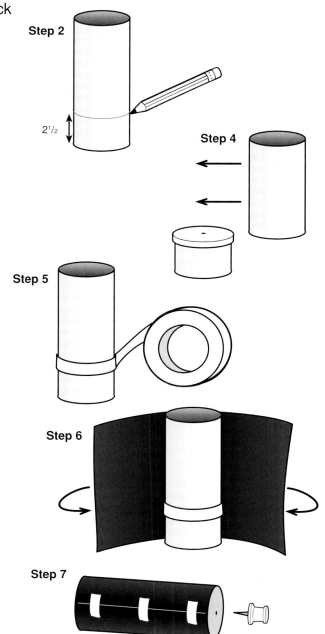

Step 2

2¹/₂

Step 4

Step 5

Step 6

Step 7

©2000 The Education Center, Inc. • *Investigating Science* • *Light & Sound* • TEC1737

Note to the teacher: Pair students. Provide each pair with a copy of this page and the materials listed. Each pair's model should show an upside-down color image of the object being viewed. Caution students not to point their models directly at the sun or other sources of light.

at eac.
line.

Refraction

Use the following activities and reproducibles to help your students better understand the bendability of light.

Lines of Light
(Demonstration)

Show your students how light travels in a straight line with this easy demonstration. Set up this demonstration in a classroom that can be darkened as much as possible. Use a pencil or other sharp object to make a small hole near the center of a sheet of black poster board. Have two students hold the poster board by its edges, careful not to block the hole. Position an overhead projector so the light from the projector will shine toward the poster board. Turn on the projector. Then gently sprinkle baby powder or flour in the air above the light beam coming in through the hole as shown. *(A beam of light traveling in a straight line should be visible.)* Explain to students that over the years scientists have debated about how light travels. Further explain that in 1905 Albert Einstein discovered that a ray of light is actually the path taken by *photons,* or light particles, that travel in a straight line. Today scientists believe that light can travel either like a particle or more like a wave, depending on the experiment conducted.

Background for the Teacher

- *Light* is an energy form that travels freely through space. Where there is nothing to delay its travel, light moves at a speed of 186,282 miles per second.
- The speed of light changes as it passes through different objects: 140,000 miles per second through water; 124,000 miles per second through glass.
- Because light travels at different speeds through different objects, it changes direction, or *bends,* when it passes from one transparent material to another. This change in direction is called *refraction.*
- Because nontransparent or opaque objects such as wood or metal do not allow light to pass through them, a shadow is cast on the opposite side of the light source.
- The study of light is called *optics.* Optics attempts to describe how light, both visible and invisible, is produced, transmitted, detected, measured, and used.

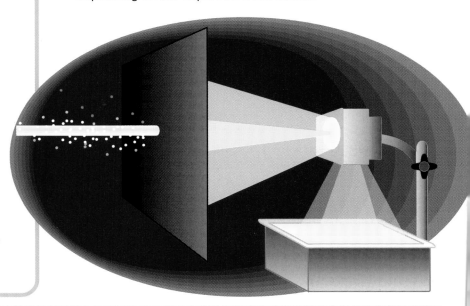

Light-Fantastic Literature

Eyewitness Science: Light by David Burnie (Dorling Kindersley Publishing, Inc.; 1992)

Light (Science Works! series) by Steve Parker (Gareth Stevens Publishing, 1997)

The Optics Book: Fun Experiments With Light, Vision, & Color by Shar Levine and Leslie Johnstone (Sterling Publishing Company, Inc.; 1998)

Shadow Play: Making Pictures With Light and Lenses (Boston Children's Museum Activity Book) by Bernie Zubrowski (Morrow Junior Books, 1995)

Does a container's shape affect how light is refracted? Your students are sure to answer "yes" after completing this easy activity. Prior to beginning this activity, create a ray box by following the directions on page 19. Also collect several different-shaped transparent containers. For example, square, round, rectangular, triangular, and flask-shaped clear decorative bottles may be used. To begin the demonstration, set up the ray box with the single-slot card positioned over the light hole. Place a large sheet of white paper on the table in front of the ray box. Have students gather around the ray box. Then turn off the classroom lights. Fill the different-shaped bottles with water, then place the bottles in front of the light beam, one at a time. Shine the light through each bottle onto the paper. Discuss with students the amount of refraction they observe as the beam passes through each bottle. Explain to students that the more a substance bends light, the larger its *refractive index,* or bending power.

Pouring Light
(Experiment)

Clue students in to the technological uses of refracted light with this enlightening activity. To begin, explain to students that light can be used to send large amounts of information long distances through glass wires called *fiber-optic cables.* The light carries data, sometimes in the form of sound and pictures, through these cables. Further explain that light is beamed into optical fibers at an angle that causes it to bounce along inside the fiber's core. The light is then reflected inside the fiber without passing out of the core. Pair students; then provide each pair with the materials listed and a copy of the directions shown. After they complete the experiment, explain to students that the light from the flashlight was reflected back and forth inside the stream of water similarly to how light moves in an optical fiber.

Materials for each pair of students: one 12-oz. Styrofoam® cup, sheet of aluminum foil, masking tape, small pitcher filled with water, bucket, flashlight

Directions:
1. Use a pencil to punch a small hole near the bottom of the Styrofoam cup as shown.
2. Form an aluminum cone around the front part of the flashlight, leaving the on/off switch clear. (The open end of the cone should be wide enough to fit around the top of the cup.) Tape the cone in place around the flashlight.
3. Place your finger over the hole in the cup. Fill the cup three-quarters full of water.
4. Put the aluminum cone over the cup. Turn on the flashlight; then turn off the light in the room.
5. Hold the cup over the bucket and remove your finger from the hole.
6. Observe the water as it flows from the cup into the bucket. *(Light should be visible in the water stream.)*

Observations:

convex:

The light was a strong point.

concave:

The light was fuzzy and not as clear.

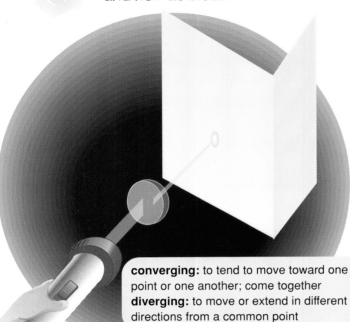

converging: to tend to move toward one point or one another; come together
diverging: to move or extend in different directions from a common point

Directions:

1. Cut off the top three inches of the milk jug. Also cut a circle three inches in diameter from a side of the jug opposite its handle. Cover the edges of the circular hole with tape.
2. Place the plastic wrap over the top of the jug, allowing it to sag slightly in the middle. Tape the plastic wrap to the sides of the jug.
3. Pour a small amount of water onto the plastic wrap.
4. Put one small object at a time through the circular hole in the jug. While holding the object in place, look at it from the top of the jug through the water.
5. Pour a larger amount of water onto the plastic wrap. Repeat Step 4 to observe any difference in the amount of magnification.
6. Discuss how the different amounts of water affect the magnification. *(There should be no noticeable difference in the amount of magnification when more water is used.)*

Focusing the Light
(Experiment)

Here's an easy activity that lets your students experiment with focusing refracted light beams using different lenses. To begin, explain to students that curved lenses can be used to bend or refract light. Further explain that some lenses focus light to a point (convex) while other lenses spread light beams out (concave). Next, pair students and provide each pair with the materials listed below and a copy of the directions shown. As a follow-up activity, have each pair write a definition for *converging* and *diverging* based on the results of this experiment. Have the pairs share their definitions with the class before reading aloud the dictionary definitions below.

Materials for each pair of students:
1 manila folder, 1 convex (converging) and concave (diverging) lens, flashlight, 8" x 12" white paper, markers or crayons, ruler

Directions:
1. Stand the folder on a desk or tabletop as shown.
2. Hold the flashlight 12–15 inches from the folder. Position one lens in front of the flashlight.
3. After the classroom lights are turned off, slowly move the lens from the flashlight toward the folder. Observe how the light beam looks as it is focused through the lens.
4. Sketch your results on the white paper and write a sentence describing how the light looked as it passed through the lens.
5. Repeat the process using the other lens.

* Check a mail-order science supply catalog for inexpensive lens kits. Most of these kits contain double convex and concave lenses which can be used for the activities in this unit.

Milk-Jug Magnifier
(Following Directions, Making Observations)

Let students see how this easy-to-assemble project uses refracted light to magnify objects, making them seem bigger than they actually are. Pair students, and give each pair the materials listed. Guide students through the steps at the left to create the magnifiers and make their observations. Follow up by having each child list three ways a water magnifier could be useful to him.

Materials for each pair of students: 1
plastic gallon-size milk jug, scissors, ruler, clear (or masking) tape, plastic cup filled with water, 8" x 8" piece of clear plastic wrap, small objects (pencil or pen, crayon, twig, sticker, etc.)

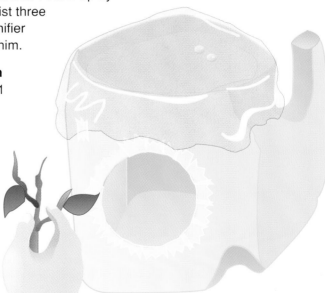

Directions:
1. Lightly coat the insides of the curved containers with nonstick cooking spray.
2. Place the curved containers in the dish of rice to keep them from tipping. Carefully pour Jell-O into each container.
3. Place the baking dish in the refrigerator for approximately three hours or until the Jell-O hardens.
4. To remove each lens from its container, place it upside down on a sheet of clear plastic wrap. If it doesn't come out, place the container in a dish of hot water for ten seconds; then try again. Repeat the hot water step until the lens slides out of the container.
5. Place one lens (still atop the plastic wrap) on a newspaper page. Lift the lens and the plastic wrap until the type on the page is magnified. In the same manner, experiment with each of the other lenses.

The Actions of Refraction Revealed

...there is ... travels freely through
...t a speed of 18... elay its travel, light
...peed of light chang... ...es per second.
...asses through
...t objects: 140,000 ... econd through
...4,000 miles ... rough glass.
...speeds through
- Be... ...irection, or bends,
different... ...om one transparent material to
when it passes ... another. This change in direction is called _refraction._
- Because nontransparent or opaque objects such
...od or metal do not allow light to pass through
...ow is cast on the opposite side
...attempts

Jell-O® Magnification
(Experiment)

Your students are sure to enjoy making these wiggly, jiggly magnifying glasses! Explain to students that when a _convex lens,_ a lens that curves outward, is held near an object, it makes the object look bigger. This is because the lens bends the rays of light inward. When we look through the lens, our eyes see those rays as straight lines, and the image seems magnified. Divide your students into small groups. Have each group make its own convex lenses with the materials listed and a copy of the directions shown.

Materials for each group: $1/2$ c. prepared Jell-O®*; hot water; 3 or 4 different-sized containers with curved bottoms, such as measuring spoons, ladles, or ice-cream scoops; nonstick cooking spray; large flat baking dish half-filled with uncooked rice; several sheets of clear plastic wrap; access to a refrigerator; newspaper page

* Prepare Jell-O by mixing four 3-ounce boxes of yellow or orange Jell-O with 4 cups of water.

Type of Lens	Convex Lens	Concave Lens
Draw the lens		
Observations	Makes things appear larger	Makes things appear smaller

Light 'n' Lenses
(Recording Observations)

Use this experiment to help students observe how different types of lenses are affected by light. Begin by explaining to students that there are two main types of lenses: convex and concave. A _convex lens_ is thicker in the middle than it is around the edges. Light passing through a convex lens is bent inward. A _concave lens_ is thicker at the edges than it is in the center. Light passing through a concave lens is bent outward. Divide students into small groups; then provide each group with a concave lens, a convex lens, a sheet of white paper, a ruler, a page of written text, and a copy of the directions shown. If desired, have groups list common objects that utilize convex or concave lenses.

Directions:
1. Copy the chart above onto white paper.
2. Sketch a picture of each type of lens in the space provided.
3. Hold each lens up to a sheet of paper with text written on it.
4. Move the lens different distances from the paper.
5. Record your observations about each type of lens.

Directions:
1. Copy the chart above onto white
2. Sketch picture of each type of ...ns in ...e space provided.
3. ...each lens up to ... sheet of paper with text ...with text ...on it.
4. Move the lens dif...erent distanc...ances from the paper.
5. Record your observations about each type of lens.

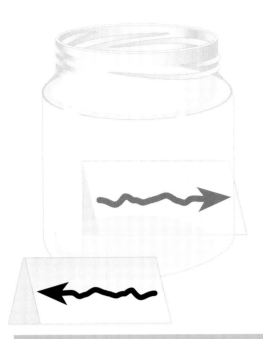

Arrow Play
(Experiment)

Can water make an arrow appear to be pointing in the opposite direction? Challenge your students to find out with this simple experiment. Divide students into small groups. Provide each group with a large index card, a black marker, and a small glass jar filled with water. Direct the group to fold the card in half as shown. Have the group draw a large left-facing arrow on one side of the index card; then stand the card up on a desk or tabletop. Next, have each group place its jar of water directly in front of the card. Instruct the group members to take turns crouching down at eye level to see the arrow through the jar of water. *(Students should see that the arrow appears to be pointing in the opposite direction.)* Explain to students that the water in the jar acts as a lens. When an object is viewed through the water lens, light waves come from each side of the object, cross inside the water lens, and appear to come out the opposite side. Have each group draw other symbols and patterns on index cards, then notice if viewing them through the water makes them appear to be backward.

Refraction Actions
(Making Observations)

Set up this series of stations so students can observe and explore *refracting* light. First, gather the materials needed for each station listed at the right. Display a card labeled with the station number at each station. Next, divide students into groups of three and give each student a copy of page 20 to complete as directed. Then have each group rotate through the stations to discover what refraction is by observing it in several different ways. After students have visited all the stations, have them discuss what they observed and agree on a definition of refraction. *(Students will observe light traveling through substances of different densities, causing it to slow down and bend instead of traveling in a straight line.)*

Station 1—clear container of water containing a pencil and a ruler, both extending above the waterline
Station 2—prism
Station 3—glass jar (such as a mayonnaise jar), any paper with words printed on it, pitcher of water
Station 4—glass microscope slide, any paper with words printed on it, plastic cup of water, eyedropper, paper towels
Station 5—2 paper towel (or bathroom tissue) rolls, 9" x 13" clear glass baking dish filled with water
Station 6—sheet of paper on which a horizontal line marked with two 3" fish shapes about 6 inches apart has been drawn, clear glass baking dish filled with water

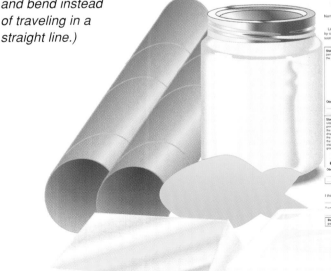

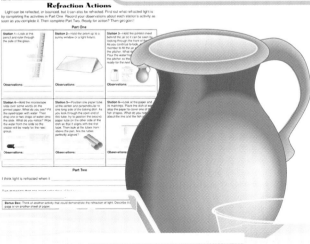

Let a Little Light Out

To study how light behaves, scientists often use a light source called a *ray box*. It produces a thin beam of light that travels in only one direction. Make your own ray box by following the directions below.

Materials: large shoebox with lid, 3 index cards, masking tape, flashlight, scissors, ruler

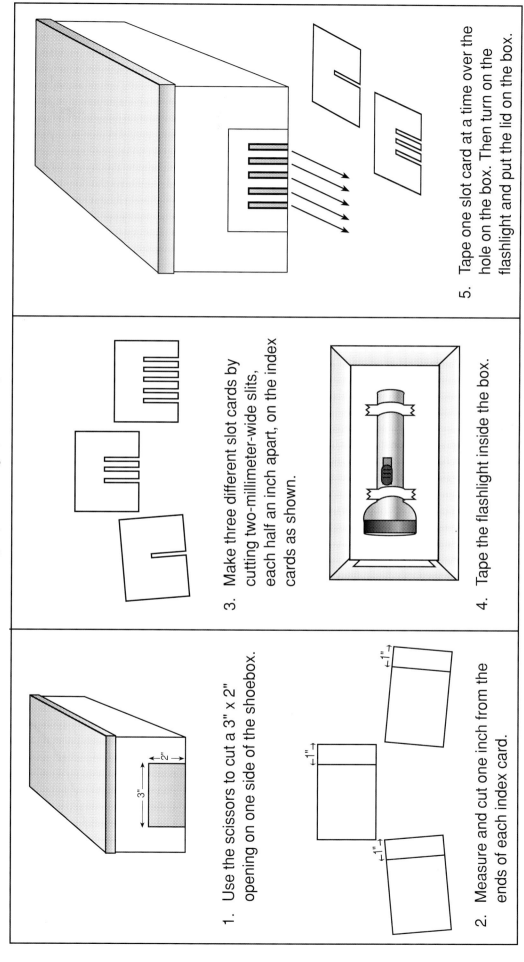

1. Use the scissors to cut a 3" x 2" opening on one side of the shoebox.

2. Measure and cut one inch from the ends of each index card.

3. Make three different slot cards by cutting two-millimeter-wide slits, each half an inch apart, on the index cards as shown.

4. Tape the flashlight inside the box.

5. Tape one slot card at a time over the hole on the box. Then turn on the flashlight and put the lid on the box.

Note to the teacher: If desired, have each student collect the materials listed and make the ray box at home. Direct the student to bring his ray box to use with "Container Consequences" on page 15.

Name ____ *Recording sheet*

Refraction Actions

Light can be reflected, or bounced, but it can also be refracted. Find out what refracted light is by completing the activities in Part One. Record your observations about each station's activity as soon as you complete it. Then complete Part Two. Ready for action? Then get goin'!

Part One

Station 1—Look at the pencil and ruler through the side of the glass.

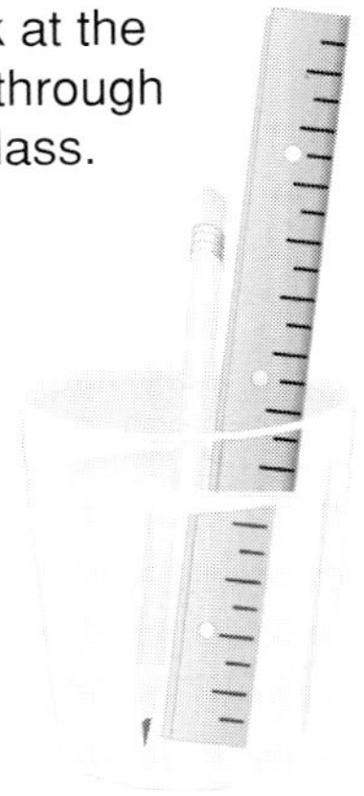

Observations: ______________________

____

____

Station 2—Hold the prism up to a sunny window or a light fixture.

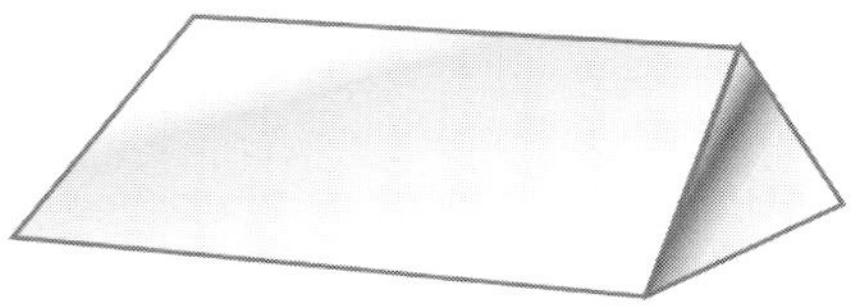

Observations: ______________________

____

____

Station 3—Hold the printed sheet behind the jar so it can be seen by looking through the front of the jar. As you continue to look, ask a group member to fill the jar with water from the pitcher. What do you notice? Pour the water from the jar back into the pitcher so the station will be ready for the next group.

Observations: ______________________

____

____

Station 4—Hold the microscope slide over some words on the printed paper. What do you see? Fill the eyedropper with water. Then drop one or two drops of water onto the slide. What do you notice? Wipe the water from the slide so the station will be ready for the next group.

Observations: ______________________

____

____

Station 5—Position one paper tube at the center and perpendicular to one long side of the baking dish. As you look through the open end of this tube, try to position the second paper tube on the other side of the dish so that it aligns with the first tube. Then look at the tubes from above the pan. Are the tubes perfectly aligned?

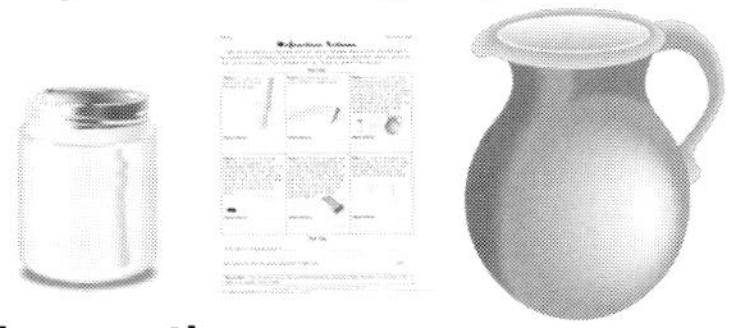

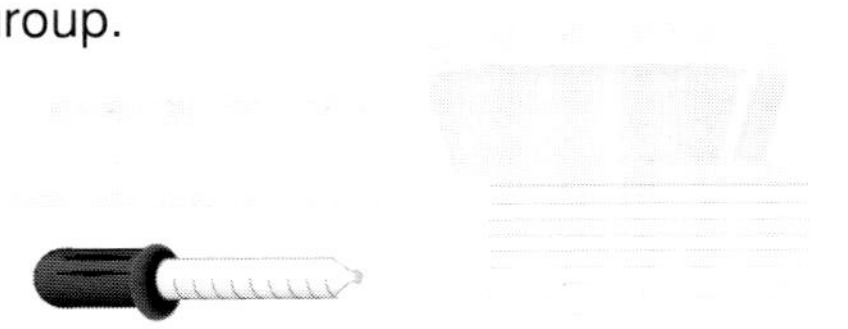

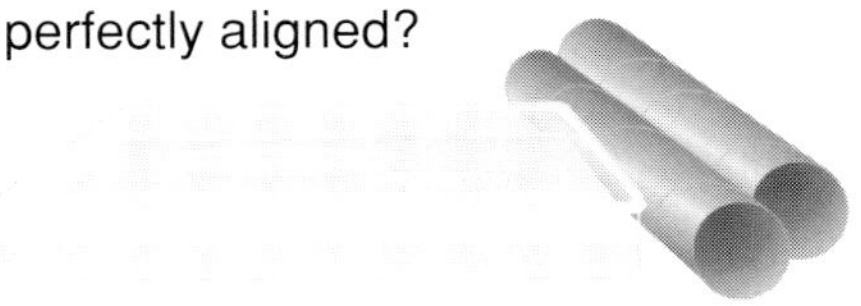

Observations: ______________________

____

____

Station 6—Look at the paper and its markings. Place the dish of water atop the paper to cover one of the fish shapes. What do you notice about the line and the fish shapes?

Observations: ______________________

____

____

Part Two

I think light is refracted when it ____

____.

Two materials that are good refractors of light are ______________________________ and

______________________________ .

Bonus Box: Think of another activity that could demonstrate the refraction of light. Describe it on the back of this page or on another sheet of paper.

 Note to the teacher: Use with "Refraction Actions" on page 18.

Money Magic

Make money appear and disappear with these light refraction tricks.

The Disappearing Penny

Materials: clear plastic cup, penny, water

Procedure:

1. Place the penny under the clear plastic cup.

2. Observe the penny through the side of the cup.

3. Then have a partner fill the cup with water.

Observation and Analysis:

What do you see? _____

_____

Why do you think you see this? _____

_____

The Appearing Penny

Materials: mini foil pie pan, penny, water

Procedure:

1. Place the penny on the bottom of the mini pie pan so that the coin is against the edge of the pan nearest you.

2. Move away from the pan until the coin is out of view.

3. Have a partner fill the pie pan with water as you watch for the penny.

Observation and Analysis:

What do you see? _____

_____

Why do you think you see this? _____

_____

©2000 The Education Center, Inc. • *Investigating Science* • *Light & Sound* • TEC1737 • Key p. 48

Note to the teacher: Pair students. Provide each pair with a copy of this page and the materials listed.

Color

Dazzle your students with this colorful collection of activities to help them recognize the close relationship between color and light.

 Background for the Teacher

- Light waves have a range of *wavelengths,* which appear as different colors.
- Light that contains all wavelengths in the same proportions as sunlight appears white and is known as *white light.*
- The longest wavelength of light that can be seen by the human eye is red. The shortest is violet. Humans cannot see *ultraviolet* or *infrared* wavelengths.
- A *spectrum* (rainbow) is produced when white light is broken into different colors.
- The human eye contains light-sensing cells called *rods* and *cones.* Each of three kinds of cones responds most strongly to a different color: blue, green, or red.
- Water droplets, bubbles, and other curved or angled surfaces *refract* (bend) white light and separate the colors into bands of light.
- *Colorants* are substances that are mixed to give color to materials such as paint, crayons, ink, and chalk. A common group of primary colorants consists of red, yellow, and blue.
- Mixing colored lights produces new colors by adding light of different wavelengths. The primary colors of light are red, green, and blue.

A Cast of Colorful Books

The Nature and Science of Color by Jane Burton and Kim Taylor (Gareth Stevens Publishing, 1998)

The Science Book of Color by Neil Ardley (Harcourt Brace Jovanovich, Publishers; 1991)

You'd Never Believe It But...A Rainbow Is a Circle and Other Facts About Color by Helen Taylor (Aladdin Books Ltd, 1999)

Split the Light Fantastic!
(Experiment)

Open your students' eyes to the colorful nature of white light with this illuminating activity. Begin by explaining that light from the sun or a lamp looks white (or appears colorless) but it actually contains all the colors of the rainbow. Further explain that when a beam of light passes through a curved or angled surface—such as a raindrop or a prism—its wavelengths are bent. The wavelengths spread out into the *visible spectrum* (rainbow) of red, orange, yellow, green, blue, indigo, and violet. Follow the steps below to demonstrate the splitting of light into the visible spectrum of colors.

Materials: 9" x 12" sheet of white poster board, ruler, scissors, clear plastic shoebox, small mirror, magnifying glass, water, class supply of drawing paper, and markers or crayons

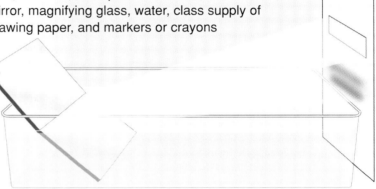

Steps:
1. Cut a 5" x ½" slit in the center of the poster board.
2. Place the mirror inside the shoebox and lean it against one end. Then pour water into the box until the mirror is covered halfway.
3. Place the box in the sunlight. Adjust the position of the box until the sun shines on the mirror.
4. Have a student volunteer hold the poster board above the box so that sunlight is shining through the slit onto the underwater part of the mirror. Adjust the mirror's angle until the rainbow's reflection appears on the poster board. *(Each wavelength bends at a different angle. When the wavelengths hit the wedge of water between the mirror and the water's surface, the colors are refracted in slightly different directions and the colors are spread out.)*
5. Have another student volunteer move the magnifying glass between the poster board and the mirror until the rainbow disappears. *(The rainbow disappears because the magnifying glass lens bends the light, blending the colors together again.)*
6. Have students create posters explaining and illustrating how the mirror, water, and light form the rainbow. Extend the activity by challenging students to add illustrations and explanations of familiar places that rainbows appear, such as bubbles, waterfalls, and compact discs (CDs).

Light-Bending Bubbles
(Experiment)

Demonstrate *refraction* of light with this simple experiment. Explain that when light hits the water in a bubble, it is split up into its different wavelengths, resulting in the colors of the rainbow. This bends the light into the spectrum of colors we call a rainbow. Divide students into groups and designate a sunny area for each group to work. Then supply each group with the materials listed and guide them through the steps below to complete the experiment.

Materials for each group of two or three students: bubble solution, wand, 2-oz. plastic cup, one 9" x 12" sheet of black construction paper, one white paper towel, sunlit work area

Steps:
1. Blow a medium-sized bubble, catch it on the wand, and then transfer it to the cup's open end. (Repeat as necessary to complete the remaining steps.)
2. Observe and record the shape and color(s) in the bubble. *(The bubble is rounded. Many colors flow and swirl on its surface.)*
3. Shield the bubble from sunlight by carefully wrapping the black construction paper around it. Observe and record the color(s) in the bubble. *(The rainbow of colors disappears without the sun's light.)*
4. Pop the bubble on the paper towel. Observe and record the result. *(The bubble will leave a wet but colorless mark on the paper towel.)*
5. Write a paragraph explaining why colors appear in bubbles that are made from a colorless solution.

Keep Your Eye on the Color
(Experiment)

Use this activity to introduce your students to *cones,* the special light-sensitive cells that enable people to see colors. Begin by explaining that cones are found at the back of the eye in the *retina.* One type of cone responds most strongly to blue light, one to green light, and a third to red light. The cones send the response messages to the brain, where they are interpreted as the color(s) being seen. Mention to students that *color blindness* (confusing certain colors or being unable to see certain colors) occurs when one type of cone is missing or not working properly.

If overused, cones can get tired and stop working briefly. When this happens, other cones help out, producing an interesting effect called an *afterimage.* Guide students through the steps below to help them understand the role of cones and the appearance of afterimages.

Materials for each student: red, blue, and green crayons or markers, eight 4" squares of white construction paper

Steps:
1. Draw and color a large blue square, green triangle, and red circle, each onto a separate construction paper square.
2. Place the red circle and a plain white square next to each other. Put the other papers out of sight.
3. Stare at the red circle for about 30 seconds. Then look directly at the white square. *(A green circle should appear on the white square after several seconds.)*
4. Repeat Steps 2 and 3 using the green triangle and blue square shapes. *(A red triangle should appear next to the green triangle, and a yellow square should appear next to the blue square.)*
5. Extend the activity by having students draw a U.S. flag on a 4" square. Substitute green for red areas, yellow for blue areas, and black for white areas. Then follow Steps 2 and 3 to see the afterimage of the flag in its true patriotic colors!

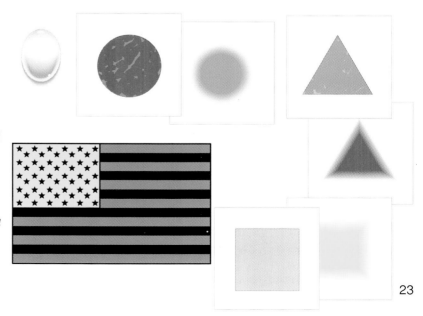

23

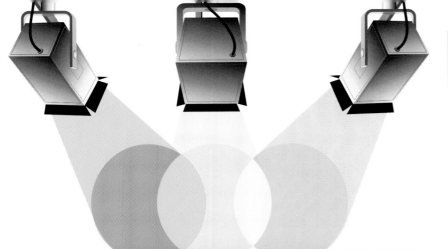

Spotlight on White Light
(Demonstration, Mixing Light Colors)

Involve students in this demonstration to show the surprising results of mixing colored lights. Explain that color *filters* let light that is the same color as the filter pass through but block out other colors. Further explain that theaters use spotlights of the primary colors of light (red, blue, and green) along with filters to create the special effects enjoyed by audiences of concerts and plays. To complete the demonstration, you will need three flashlights of equal brightness; three six-inch paper tubes; three rubber bands; red, green, and blue cellophane sheets; and an area of white wall space. Attach the cellophane to the tubes with rubber bands. Darken the room as much as possible. Then select three student volunteers to shine the flashlights through the tubes onto the wall. Invite students to suggest various combinations of the colored lights. Guide students to conclude that red and green make yellow light, red and blue make magenta light, and blue and green make *cyan* (aqua) light. Ask students to predict which color might result from mixing all three light colors. Then have the volunteers shine all three lights on the same spot. Were the students surprised to see that red, green, and blue lights make white light?

Cool Color Spinner
(Making a Color Wheel)

For additional reinforcement of the concept that white light is made of colors, have each student create his own cool color spinner. To complete this activity, each student will need one tagboard copy of page 25; a 24" length of strong, thin string; crayons; scissors; and a sharpened pencil. Remind students that the visible spectrum consists of seven different-colored wavelengths of white light. In order, the colors are red, orange, yellow, green, blue, indigo, and violet. Turn off the lights in your classroom and shine light from an overhead projector or flashlight through a prism onto the wall. Ask students how the prism proves that white light is made of the rainbow colors. *(When light passes through the prism, it bends and splits the light into the colors of the spectrum.)* Next, give each student a copy of page 25 and review the directions. Allow time for students to make the disks. When the disks are finished, divide students into pairs. Have one student in each pair loop the string around his index fingers while the partner turns the wheel repeatedly in the same direction to twist the thread tightly. Then have both students stare at the colored side of the wheel as it is released. *(The wheel spins too fast for the eyes to see each color separately. The seven colors blend together and appear yellowish white.)*

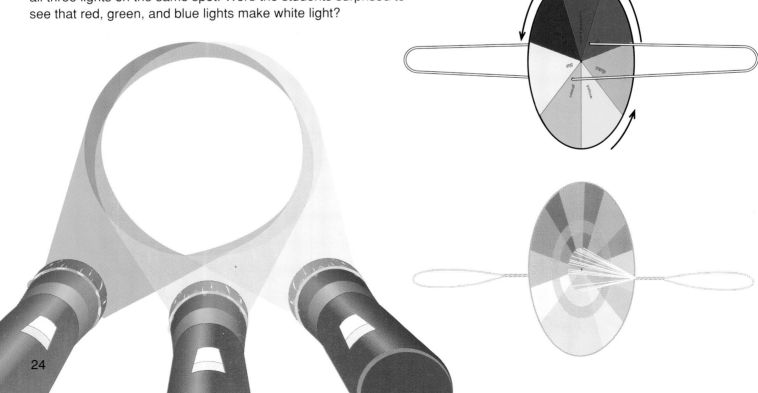

Spinning White Light

Follow the steps below to create a color spinner that will blend the seven colors of the rainbow back into white.

Materials: 7 crayons: red, orange, yellow, green, blue, indigo (blue plus purple), and violet (purple); scissors; 24" of strong, thin string; sharpened pencil

Steps:

1. Color each section of the wheel using the colors shown.
2. Cut out the wheel. Using a pencil, carefully poke two small holes in the center of the wheel as shown (Figure 1).
3. Thread the string through the holes and tie the ends together. Center the circle on the string (Figure 2).
4. Follow your teacher's directions to make the spinner blend the rainbow of colors into white (Figure 3).

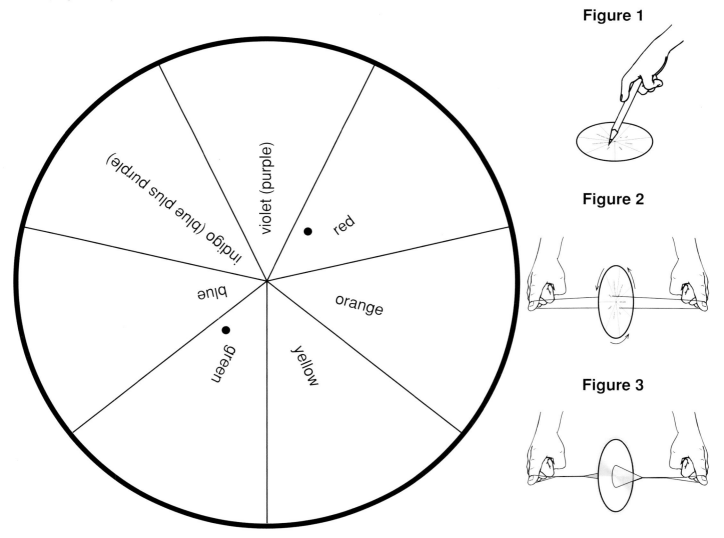

Figure 1

Figure 2

Figure 3

The color wheel sections labeled: violet (purple), red, orange, yellow, green, blue, indigo (blue plus purple)

Bonus Box: Make small wheels with primary color combinations such as blue and yellow, red and blue, and red and yellow. Spin these to discover the secondary colors.

Starring Secondary Colors!

Red, yellow, and blue make up one group of *primary* colors. When they are combined in pairs, they produce *secondary* colors. Follow the directions below to create a sparkling star of primary and secondary colors.

Materials: one 4" x 8" sheet each of red, yellow, and blue cellophane; 1 sheet of white copy paper; ballpoint pen; scissors; glue stick

Directions:

1. Cut out the pattern below. Using a ballpoint pen, trace the pattern onto each color of cellophane. Cut out the pieces and lay aside.
2. Fold the white paper in half. Place the pattern on the fold. Trace and cut out the pattern, being careful not to cut the fold (Figure 1).
3. Fold the folded pattern in thirds to form a diamond shape. Then fold it in half again (Figure 2).
4. Snip designs into the long side of the triangle, being careful not to cut off the pointed ends (Figure 3). Carefully open the star.
5. Rub the glue stick on the white paper star. Fit the blue cellophane cutout onto one section of the star, being careful to line up points. Using the diagram as a guide (Figure 4), fit the yellow cellophane cutout on the star. Then add the red cellophane cutout as shown.
6. Display your star in the classroom window, where it will cast primary and secondary colors into the room.

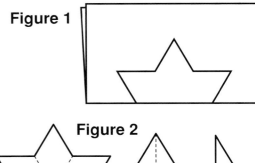

Figure 1

Figure 2

Figure 3

Figure 4

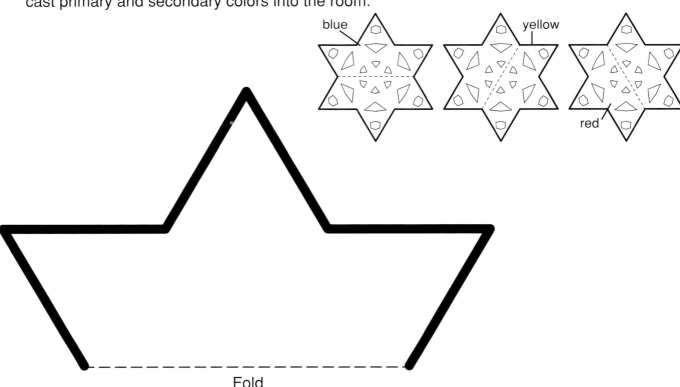

Fold

What's Your Favorite Color?

Survey fellow students to find out which rainbow colors have the most remarkable ratings. Follow the steps below to complete the activity.

A. Survey each student in your class to find out which color of the rainbow is his or her favorite. Record a tally mark for each student in the appropriate crayon on the table below.

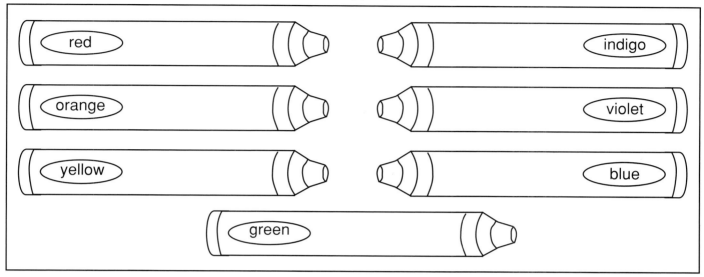

B. Use the results from the table above to create a bar graph. Remember to complete the following steps:

1. Label the grid's horizontal axis and vertical axis.
2. Look at your class's data and determine what your scale should be. (Choose a scale with an appropriate interval. Be sure all of your bars will fit on the grid provided.)
3. Construct a different bar for each color.
4. Write a title for your graph.

Sound

*Use this collection of experiments, activities,
and reproducibles to amplify your study of sound!*

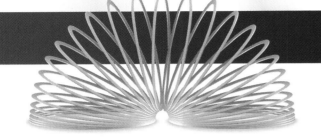

Slinky® Sound Waves
(Demonstration, Sound Waves, Pitch)

Help students see and hear how sound waves move with this Slinky® activity. Share with students the definition of sound waves from this page, pointing out that in this case the sound waves will be traveling from spring to spring. Next, divide students into groups of three and give them the materials listed below. Then guide them through the steps that follow.

Materials for each group: 1 full-sized metal Slinky® toy, two 18" lengths of string, 2 paper cups, 2 small paper clips, sharpened pencil

Steps:

1. Direct one member from each group to carefully poke a small hole in the bottom of each of the cups using a sharpened pencil. To make earphones, have the student put one end of each string through the hole in the bottom of each cup, securing the end of the string that is inside the cup around a paper clip (as shown below).
2. Direct two students to each take an end of the Slinky and stretch it until it is about six feet in length.
3. Instruct the third student to tie the earphones to the Slinky's center about a foot apart (as shown below).
4. Have the student hold the earphones up to her ears. Next, have one of the students holding an end of the Slinky lightly pluck or tap the spring. *(Explain to students that this will cause vibrations to travel along the Slinky. The waves will not look like waves in an ocean. Instead, one coil will bump into another, causing domino-like waves.)*
5. Ask the student with the earphones to describe the sounds she hears.
6. After the spring has stopped vibrating, have one of the students holding the Slinky tap or pluck the spring quickly several times so that the waves are closer together. Then have the same student tap the spring more slowly so the waves are farther apart. Again ask the student in the middle what she hears. *(The student should respond that she heard a high-pitched sound and then a low-pitched sound. Explain that this is because the* frequency, *or number of vibrations, influences the* pitch, *or how high or low the sound is. When the spring is plucked quickly, the vibrations are closer together, causing a higher pitch. When the spring is plucked slowly, the vibrations are farther apart, causing a lower pitch.)*
7. Have group members trade places and repeat the experiment.

Background for the Teacher

- *Sound* is a form of energy. Each sound that we hear is caused by vibrations.
- *Sound waves* occur when vibrations pass from one molecule of a gas, liquid, or solid to another.
- *Acoustics* is the science of sound and its effects on people.
- *Frequency*—measured in *hertz*—is the number of vibrations made by a vibrating object per second. *Noise* is sound with many random frequencies.
- *Intensity*—measured in *decibels*—relates to the amount of energy flowing in sound waves.
- *Pitch* is the degree of highness or lowness of a sound.
- *Amplitude* is the distance that a vibrating object moves from its position of rest as it vibrates.
- A *conductor* is any substance through which sound can travel.

One Boomin' Booklist!

Communications and Broadcasting (Milestones in Discovery and Invention series) by Harry Henderson (Facts on File, Inc.; 1997)

Music (Eyewitness Books series) by Neil Ardley (Alfred A. Knopf, Inc.; 1989)

Sounds All Around (Let's-Read-and-Find-Out Science® series) by Wendy Pfeffer (HarperCollins Publishers, Inc.; 1999)

A Spoonful of Sound
(Experiment, Pitch, Frequency)

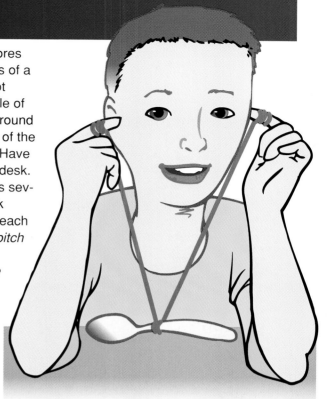

Give your students a spoonful of sound with an experiment that explores pitch. Explain to students that *pitch* is the degree of highness or lowness of a sound. Pair students and give each pair one metal spoon and a four-foot length of string. Have one student in each pair tie the spoon in the middle of the string as shown. Instruct the student to wind the ends of the string around each of his pointer fingers, making sure the string is even on both sides of the spoon. Direct the student to carefully place a pointer finger in each ear. Have the other student swing the spoon so that it gently strikes the edge of a desk. Next, have the student shorten the string by winding it around his fingers several more times. Then have the other student strike the edge of the desk again. Direct the second student in each pair to try the experiment. Ask each pair how the two sounds compared. *(Students should respond that the pitch was lower when the string was longer and higher when the string was shorter. Explain to students that pitch is determined by* frequency, *or the number of vibrations made by a vibrating object in one second. Further explain that the longer string caused a lower pitch because fewer vibrations were able to reach the ear in one second. The shorter string caused a higher pitch because more vibrations reached the ear in one second.)* If desired, allow students to experiment with varying lengths of string to compare the differences in pitch.

Dancing Sound
(Demonstration, Sound Vibrations)

Strike a beat with this simple demonstration exploring sound waves and vibrations. First, gather a small plastic bowl, plastic wrap, a large rubber band, puffed wheat cereal or about a tablespoon of sand, a cookie sheet, a wooden spoon, and a radio. Cover the opening of the bowl with plastic wrap, pulling it taut. Secure it with a rubber band as shown. Place the cereal or sand on the plastic wrap. Holding the cookie sheet several inches away from the bowl, strike it several times with the spoon. Ask students what they observe happening to the cereal. Next, place the radio several inches from the bowl and turn it on. Again ask students what they observe happening to the cereal. *(Students should respond that the cereal seemed to "dance" each time the cookie sheet was struck or the radio was turned on.)* Ask students what they think caused the cereal to dance. *(The cereal appeared to dance when the plastic wrap vibrated due to the sound waves produced by the spoon striking the pan and the sound waves coming from the radio. When objects vibrate, they make the surrounding air vibrate, as shown by the dancing cereal.)*

Listen to This!
(Experiments, Amplification)

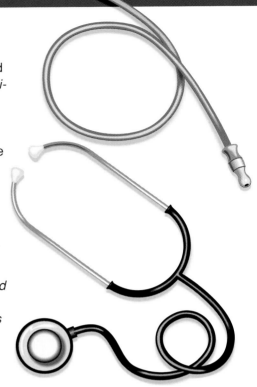

Help students gain a better understanding of amplification with these hands-on experiments. Explain to students that throughout history, devices have been created to help capture sound waves and direct them closer together, making them easier to hear. French physician René Laënnec invented the stethoscope in 1819 to listen to a patient's heart. This simple device *amplified,* or made louder, the quiet sounds within the body. Then, in 1906, the development of the "Audion" vacuum tube amplifier by Lee de Forest led the way to the development of electronic amplification.

Give each student a copy of page 35. Divide the class into pairs. Next, give each pair one plastic funnel, about one foot of plastic tubing (with a diameter of a half inch), a sheet of poster board, scissors, and tape. Then have each pair complete page 35 as directed to learn more about the stethoscope, megaphone, and ear trumpet.

After each pair has completed page 35, discuss the results. *(In the first experiment, each student should observe that she could hear the heart beating. This is because the stethoscope amplified the sound of the heart. In the second experiment, the student should observe that she could hear the sound better and her voice was made louder by using the cone. When the cone is used to send sound, it holds the sound waves together, preventing the waves from spreading in the air too quickly. When the cone is used to listen, it collects and funnels the sound waves to the ear, thus amplifying the sounds.*

Figure 1

Bouncing Sound
(Experiment, Reflecting Sound)

Sound travels. Sound makes waves. But does sound bounce, too? Help students find out with this hands-on experiment. Divide students into groups of three. Then give each group the materials listed below and guide students through the steps that follow.

Materials for each group: 2 empty wrapping paper tubes, a small bell, one 12" x 12" piece of cardboard, 1 small pillow

Steps:

Figure 2

1. Have Student 1 hold the cardboard vertically on a table and place one tube at an angle in front of it (Figure 1).
2. Instruct Student 2 to place the other tube at the opposite angle to form a V-shape (Figure 2).
3. Direct Student 3 to sit with her back to the tube on the left and one ear against the tube on the right. Have the student cover her other ear with her hand (Figure 3).
4. Have Student 2 jingle the bell into the tube on the left. Tell Student 3 to raise her hand when she hears the bell.
5. Instruct Student 1 to trade the cardboard for the pillow. Then direct the group to repeat Steps 3 and 4.
6. Have group members trade places until each student has had a chance to listen to the bell reflected off both objects.

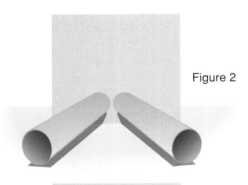

Figure 3

7. Discuss the groups' observations as a class. *(Students should conclude that the sound of the bell bounced, or reflected, off the cardboard and the pillow, but that the cardboard reflected the sound better. Explain that a hard, smooth surface (cardboard) reflects sound better than an uneven, soft surface (pillow). This is because the soft surface absorbs most of the sound.)*
8. If desired, allow students to try this experiment several times, checking to see if different sounds, such as an alarm clock or ticking watch, will reflect off the cardboard and pillow.

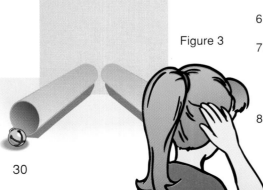

Sound Through Solids
(Experiment, Conductors)

Can sound travel through a solid, such as wood? Help students find the answer to this question with the following center activity. Explain to students that *conductors* are objects that allow sound to travel through them. Then, in a center, place a class supply of page 36, a plastic ruler, a wooden ruler, a pencil, a sponge, a jacket or cloth item, and an egg carton. Direct students to visit the center in pairs and complete page 36 as directed. *(Students should conclude that they were able to hear the sounds through the table better than through the air. Explain that this is because solid materials, such as wooden desks, are good conductors of sound.)*

Through Air and Water
(Demonstration, Conductors)

Continue your study of sound conductors with this demonstration. Remind students that a *conductor* is any substance that allows sound to travel through it. Next, pair students. Give each pair two balloons—one filled three-fourths full of water and one filled with air. Have each student, in turn, hold the water-filled balloon up to his ear and tap the balloon lightly. Direct each student to do the same with the air-filled balloon. Ask each student if he can hear the tapping through the balloons. *(Students should respond that they could hear the tapping. Explain that this is because water and air are both conductors of sound.)* If desired, have students listen to additional sounds through the balloons—such as talking, music, or clapping—to further prove that water and air are good conductors of sound.

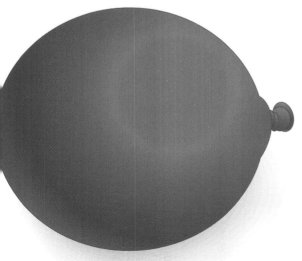

Fascinating Facts
- With the use of underwater microphones, a small explosion was heard from over 4,000 miles away. The explosion occurred off South Africa and was heard off the coast of South America!
- Whales keep in contact with each other by singing songs, which travel hundreds of miles through the sea.

Classroom Concerto
(Making Instruments)

Conduct a classroom concerto with this compilation of crafty instruments your students create! About a week before beginning this activity, gather the supplies listed below. Next, brainstorm with students different musical instruments. Discuss how you might create an instrument with everyday items, such as a shoebox, a soup can, or a comb. Have each student choose a musical instrument to make from the list below. Then give each student a copy of page 37 and the materials needed to make her instrument. After all the instruments have been made, have the class prepare a song and hold a concert for another class!

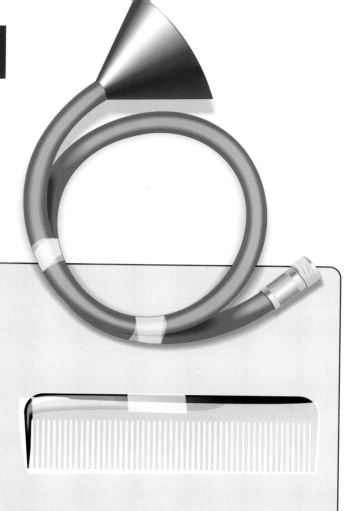

Materials:

Tambourine—foil pie pan, paper clips, hole puncher, arts-and-crafts supplies

French Horn—funnel, tape, 5' hose section with faucet attachment (cut a 10' hose in half to make two horns)

Drum—plastic bowl, plastic wrap, rubber band, eraser-topped pencil

Rattle—clean, empty plastic soda bottle with lid; rice, beans, or small rocks; arts-and-crafts supplies

Xylophone—4 or 5 same-sized glasses, water, spoon

Panpipe—4–8 straws, tape, scissors

Bottle Organ—5 same-sized plastic soda bottles, water

Guitar—sturdy shoebox, rubber bands with different widths, arts-and-crafts supplies

Kazoo—small comb, waxed paper, tape, scissors

Sounds From the Radio
(Creating a Radio Play)

Challenge your students to create believable sound effects for a radio play—just like in the old radio shows! First, gather a tape recorder, a blank tape, a recording of an old radio show (check your local library), a read-aloud play, and items for making sound effects (for example, two coconut halves, a bendable metal sheet, and a kitchen blender). Next, have students listen to a recording of a radio show. Discuss the methods and materials students think were used to create the different sounds. Then read a play aloud with the class, instructing students to note places where sound effects could be included. Discuss different ways to make those sounds. For example, hooves clomping can be made by clapping coconut shells together and a metal sheet can sound like thunder. Practice the play several times to make the sound effects sound as realistic as possible. Finally, use a tape player to record your play. If desired, invite other classes to listen to your radio play and then guess what items were used to create the sounds.

Super "Sonar-ramas"
(Making Dioramas, Creative Thinking)

Slip your students into thoughts of the deep sea with this "sonar-rific" art activity! Before beginning this activity, have each student bring in a shoebox. Next, explain to students that *sonar* stands for **so**und **n**avigation **a**nd **r**anging. Further explain that sonar uses sound waves to detect submarines, schools of fish, and other underwater objects. Instruct students to think about what they would want to detect in the ocean, such as whales, dolphins, or objects on the ocean floor. Then direct each student to use arts-and-crafts supplies and her shoebox to create a "sonar-rama" showing the ocean, the ocean floor, and what she would want to detect. If desired, have each student share her "sonar-rama" with the class, explaining what the sonar is detecting in her display.

Ingenious Innovators
(Research, Innovators of Sound)

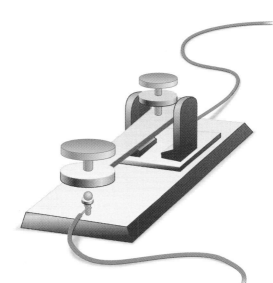

Who's responsible for what we know about sound? Help students find out with this student-created display of famous innovators. First, pair students and have each pair choose one of the famous innovators from the box below. Give each pair one sheet of 9" x 12" light-colored construction paper, a compass, scissors, and glue. Direct each pair to research its innovator to find out what contributions he made to the understanding of sound. Then have each pair cut three $4\frac{1}{2}$" diameter circles out of construction paper. On one of the circles, instruct the pair to write the innovator's name and their names. On another circle, have the pair write the facts about the innovator in paragraph form (Figure 1). Then direct the pair to fold the two circles that have been written on in half. Instruct the pair to glue half of the back of one folded circle to half of the back of the other folded circle (Figure 2). Then glue the two circles to the remaining circle (Figure 3). Display students' 3-D circles on a bulletin board titled "Ingenious Innovators."

Alexander Graham Bell
Christian Doppler
Heinrich Hertz
Thomas Edison
René Laënnec
Emile Berliner
Ernst Mach
Hermann Helmholtz
Ernst Chladni
Edwin Armstrong
John Bardeen
Walter Brattain
William Shockley
Lee de Forest

Figure 1

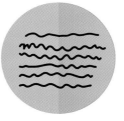

Figure 2

Figure 3

Zip, Bang, Boom!
(Onomatopoeia, Writing Poetry)

Turn your students into "onomato-poets" with this activity combining onomatopoeia and poetry. Explain to students that using a word that imitates a sound—such as *honk, beep, chatter, hiss, scream, zoom,* and *buzz*—is called *onomatopoeia.* Next, have students sit quietly in the cafeteria or classroom and listen to the sounds around them. Direct them to think of words to imitate the sounds they hear, such as *click, hum, whir, whoosh,* and *tick.* Have student volunteers share other words that imitate sounds. List students' responses on a chalkboard or a sheet of chart paper. Then instruct each student to use onomatopoeia in writing a *free verse poem,* or a poem without a particular form or rhyming scheme, on a sheet of construction paper. On the back of the sheet, have each student replace each onomatopoeic word and the surrounding words with an illustration as shown. Allow each student to trade papers with a partner to figure out the partner's illustrations.

The crocodile snarled just before splashing through the water.

The zebra sighed just before zipping through the grass.

The monkey screeched just before swishing through the trees.

And I giggled just before waking from my dream!

Double the Fun!
(Sound Review Game)

Double up on the learning and the fun with a sound review game that encourages teamwork! Begin by leading a discussion on the elements of sound that you have been studying. Next, have each student write a question that pertains to sound and its answer on a slip of paper. Collect the slips. Then determine which questions you will use and the number of points a team must earn to win the game. Divide students into two teams and have each team stand in a line on either side of the classroom. Place a bell on a desk in the center of the room where it can be easily reached by both teams. Read one of the questions aloud. Direct the first student on each team to quickly confer with her teammates about the answer, and then go to the desk and ring the bell. If the first student to ring the bell answers correctly, award her team five points. If she answers incorrectly, allow the first student from the other team to answer. If the student on the opposing team answers correctly, award her team double the number of points (ten). Have the first students go to the back of the lines, and continue to play the game until one team earns the winning number of points. Reward the team with a treat such as double minutes of free-reading time or recess!

Listen to This!

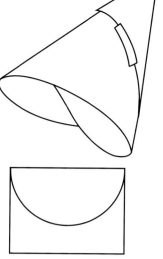

I. Follow the directions below to make a simple *stethoscope*, or listening tube.

II. Follow the directions below to make a simple ear trumpet/megaphone.

Steps:

1. Push one end of a piece of plastic tubing tightly over the spout of a funnel.

2. Record your *hypothesis*, or what you think will happen when the funnel is placed on your partner's chest with the other end next to your ear.
_____
_____
_____

3. Have your partner place the funnel end of the stethoscope on his or her chest. Place the other end up to your ear.

4. Record your *observations*, or what you heard through the tubing.
_____
_____
_____

5. Write your *conclusion*, or why you think you were able to hear what you heard.
_____
_____
_____

6. Trade places with your partner and repeat the experiment.

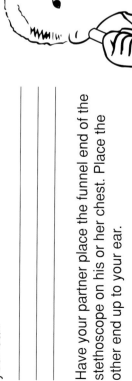

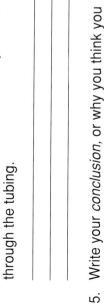

Steps:

1. Draw a half circle on a piece of poster board, cut it out, roll it into a cone, and tape it in place.

2. Record your *hypothesis*, or what you think will happen when you put the cone to your ear and listen. Then record what you think will happen when you put the cone to your mouth and speak through it.
_____

3. Ask your partner to stand about six feet away and speak to you in a normal voice. Listen to the loudness of his voice.

4. Place the small end of the cone carefully up to your ear and listen again. Is there a difference in loudness?
_____

5. Record your *observations*, or what you heard with and without the cone up to your ear. Did the cone amplify the sound of your partner's voice?
_____

6. Speak to your partner in a regular voice. Place the small end of the cone up to your mouth and repeat what you said. Did your partner notice a difference in the loudness of your voice?

7. Record your partner's observations, or what he heard with and without the cone up to your mouth. Did the cone amplify the sound of your voice?
_____

8. Trade places with your partner and repeat the experiment.

©2000 The Education Center, Inc. • *Investigating Science • Light & Sound* • TEC1737

Note to the teacher: Use with "Listen to This!" on page 30.

Name _____

Sound Through Solids

Some materials allow sound to travel through them easily. These are called *conductors*. Follow the steps below to learn more about solids as sound conductors.

A. 1. Put your head down on the desk so that one ear is on the desk. Cover your other ear with your hand.

2. Have your partner place one of the objects from the chart on the desk. Then have your partner use a pencil to tap it.

3. Listen carefully. How well does the sound travel through the desk?

4. Lift your head and listen as your partner taps the object once again. How well does the sound travel through the air?

5. On the chart, rate the loudness of each of the sounds.

6. Repeat Steps 1–5 for each of the objects on the chart.

7. Have your partner choose two additional objects to test. In the last two spaces on the chart, record the name of the object and then rate how well you could hear it.

8. Trade places with your partner and repeat Steps 1–7.

B. On the back of this sheet, explain why you think you got the ratings you did on the chart. Keep in mind what you have learned about the way sound travels.

Object	Sound Through Solid						Sound Through Air					
	not at all				very well		not at all				very well	
	0	1	2	3	4	5	0	1	2	3	4	5
plastic ruler	0	1	2	3	4	5	0	1	2	3	4	5
wooden ruler	0	1	2	3	4	5	0	1	2	3	4	5
sponge	0	1	2	3	4	5	0	1	2	3	4	5
jacket/cloth	0	1	2	3	4	5	0	1	2	3	4	5
egg carton	0	1	2	3	4	5	0	1	2	3	4	5
	0	1	2	3	4	5	0	1	2	3	4	5

©2000 The Education Center, Inc. • *Investigating Science • Light & Sound* • TEC1737

Note to the teacher: Use with "Sound Through Solids" on page 31.

Classroom Concerto

Bottle Organ

Fill the plastic bottles with different amounts of water. Blow across the top of each one to play.

Tambourine

Punch holes around the rim of a pie pan. Attach a paper clip to each hole and then add decorations to the pie pan. Shake the tambourine to play.

Xylophone

Fill each glass with a different amount of water. Tap each glass lightly with a spoon to play.

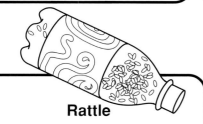

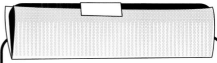

Rattle

Place rice, beans, or pebbles inside a plastic bottle. Put the lid on securely. Decorate the bottle with arts-and-crafts supplies. Shake the rattle to play.

Drum

Stretch a piece of plastic wrap tightly across the opening of a bowl. Secure the sides with a rubber band. Beat lightly with an eraser-topped pencil to play.

Kazoo

Cut the waxed paper so that it wraps around the comb once. Tape the waxed paper so the comb doesn't fall out. Press your lips lightly against the teeth of the comb and say *do* or *da* several times to play.

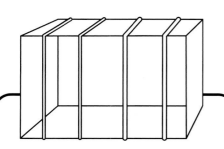
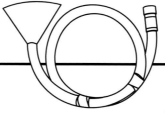
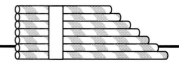

Guitar

Place several rubber bands of different widths around a shoebox, with thicker ones at one end and thinner ones at the other end. Decorate the box with arts-and-crafts supplies. Pluck the rubber bands to play.

French Horn

Attach the funnel to the end of the hose without the faucet attachment (mouthpiece), loop the tube to make a circle, and tape the circle in place. Have your teacher cut a small hole in the tube close to the mouthpiece. To play, blow into the mouthpiece while covering and uncovering the hole with your finger.

Panpipe

Cut the straws so that each one is a half inch shorter than the next one. Lay the straws in order by height and tape them together. Hold the level end of the straws against your lower lip and blow across the top of each straw to play.

©2000 The Education Center, Inc. • *Investigating Science* • *Light & Sound* • TEC1737

Detecting Decibels

Detective Dessie Bell has lost all of the sounds from the chart below. Use your detective skills to help Dessie Bell put her sounds back in order!

Directions: The chart below contains nine decibel levels, but the name of a sound made at each level is missing. Read each clue below to figure out where each sound belongs. Then write the name of the sound in the corresponding space on the chart. **Remember:** A *decibel (dB)* is used to measure the intensity level of a sound.

(Decibel Levels)

140	_____
120	_____
100	_____
90	_____
80	_____
70	_____
60	_____
20	_____
0	_____

Clues:

1. The *threshold of audibility* is the level of the weakest sound that can be heard by the human ear.
2. The *threshold of pain* is the level of the loudest sound that can be heard and may cause pain in the ear.
3. A *telephone ring* is more intense than a *conversation,* but not as intense as a *vacuum cleaner.*
4. *Heavy traffic* is more intense than a *vacuum cleaner,* but not as intense as a *circular saw.*
5. An *amplified rock concert* is more intense than a *circular saw,* but not as intense as the sound of a *jet takeoff at close range,* which is at the same level as the threshold of pain.
6. A *whisper* is not as intense as a *conversation.*

Bonus Box: Think about the numbers that are missing from the chart, such as 10, 30, and 40. On the back of this sheet, make a new chart, including the missing numbers. Then fill in the rest of the chart with sounds you think might fit at each level.

©2000 The Education Center, Inc. • *Investigating Science • Light & Sound* • TEC1737 • Key p. 48

I've Got Your Frequency

Frequency, measured in *hertz,* is the number of vibrations made by a vibrating object per second. Humans can make sound frequencies from 85 to 1,100 hertz. Some animals can emit higher frequencies than humans, and some can emit lower frequencies than humans. Study the frequency chart below and then answer the questions that follow.

Frequency Chart	
Animal	**Hertz Range**
Cat	760–1,520
Grasshopper	7,000–100,000
Bat	10,000–120,000
Dog	452–1,080
Dolphin	7,000–120,000
Human	85–1,100
Robin	2,000–13,000

Questions:

1. Which animal has the lowest frequency range? _____
   Which two have the highest? _____
   (Hint: Look at the first number for lowest and the last number for highest.)

2. Which animal has the widest frequency range? _____
   (Hint: Subtract the lowest number from the highest number for each animal.)

3. Which animal has the narrowest frequency range? _____
   (Hint: Solve the same way as in number 2.)

4. How much wider is a bat's frequency range than a human's frequency range (in hertz)?

   _____

5. How much wider is a cat's frequency range than a dog's frequency range (in hertz)?

   _____

6. Name the animals that have a wider frequency range than a human has. _____

   _____

Bonus Box: On the back of this sheet, list the animals in order from widest frequency range to narrowest frequency range.

Hearing and the Ear

Hear ye! Hear ye! Use the activities and reproducibles in this unit to explore the basics of hearing and the ear.

Background for the Teacher

- Hearing is one of the most important senses. The organ of hearing, the *ear,* is made up of three parts: the *outer ear,* the *middle ear,* and the *inner ear.*
- The outer ear is made up of the *pinna* (the visible ear) and the external ear canal. The pinna collects sound waves and funnels them into the ear canal.
- The *eardrum* is located at the end of the ear canal, separating the outer ear and the middle ear.
- There are three small bones in the middle ear: the *hammer,* the *anvil,* and the *stirrup.*
- The inner ear is made up of delicate and complex passages: the *vestibule,* the *semicircular canals,* and the *cochlea.*
- Sound waves cause *hair cells,* tiny sense cells with hairlike projections, in the inner ear to move. The hairlike cells brush against the end of the *auditory nerve,* which changes the sound wave into a signal called a nerve impulse. The brain then translates the impulses as sound.

Hearing Things?
(Listening, Recording)

Help students become aware of the many sounds surrounding them with this simple activity. First, ask the class to remain perfectly quiet for one full minute, listening for every sound. Then tell students to list all the sounds they heard during that minute. Discuss what they heard. Did students hear the same sounds? Did they notice sounds they usually don't? Why? Encourage students to try this activity at home.

Let's Hear It for Books!

Bizarre & Beautiful Ears by Santa Fe Writers Group (John Muir Publications, 1994)

Experiment With Senses by Monica Byles (Two-Can Publishing Limited, 1992)

Helen Keller by Margaret Davidson (Scholastic Inc., 1997)

Signing for Kids by Mickey Flodin (The Berkley Publishing Group, 1991)

Sound Fundamentals: Funtastic Science Activities for Kids (Fundamentals series) by Robert W. Wood (McGraw-Hill, 1997)

Let's Get Outer Ear!
(Experiment)

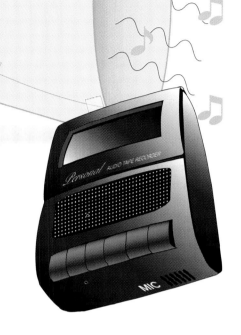

It's as plain as the nose on your face—ears are different! Some ears are small and some are big. Some earlobes are attached and some are not attached. But no matter their differences, all ears are created for the same purpose. Ask students what they think the main purpose of the outer ear, or *pinna,* is *(to collect sound).* Ask them to think about what they could do to help the pinna collect more sound than it does. Write student suggestions on the board. Next, give each student a sheet of card stock and direct the student to roll the paper into a funnel and then tape it in place. Have students trim the wide end so that it's even. Play some music for the class. Then direct students to place their funnels to their ears and replay the music at the same volume. Ask students if they noticed that the music was louder. Ask them if other sounds were louder too. Then challenge students to explain why the sound was louder with the funnels. *(More sound waves are collected in the larger area of the funnel.)*

A Different Drummer
(Experiment)

Sound waves beat out cool rhythms and soothing sounds. But if not for the *eardrum,* a thin skin covering the end of the ear canal, we wouldn't be able to hear any of them. Drum up some learning on how the eardrum receives sound and relays it to the brain with this activity. Have each student bring in a cardboard paper towel or toilet paper tube from home. Then give each student a balloon, scissors, and a rubber band. Direct the student to cut the balloon to make a piece large enough to fit over the end of the tube. Instruct the student to stretch the balloon over one end of the tube and use the rubber band to secure it in place. Have the student speak into the uncovered end of the tube while his fingers are lightly placed on the balloon-covered end of the tube. Ask students to share what happens and how it's like the eardrum and hearing. *(Explain to students that the tube acts like the ear canal, conducting sound waves, and the balloon acts like the eardrum, vibrating when the sound waves hit it. The vibrations of the eardrum are then funneled toward the hole in the middle of the ear.)*

41

Turn, Turn, Turn
(Demonstration)

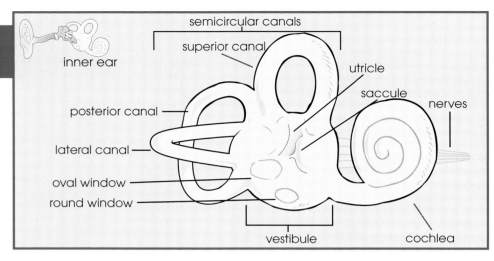

An amusement park ride, a car, and a boat are places where motion sickness can turn up. Ask your students to raise their hands if they have ever experienced motion sickness. Explain to students that the ear not only lets you hear, but it also makes balance possible. Further explain that when these balance organs are overwhelmed with motion, they can cause dizziness and some-times even nausea, or *motion sickness.* Take your class outside to a grassy area. Have two or three volunteers spin in place ten times. Have the class watch what the spinning does to the volunteers' balance. Have students observe whether the spinners can stand up straight immediately after spinning. Direct the spinners to explain how they felt when the motion stopped. *(Explain to students that the vestibular organs include the semicircular canals, utricle, and saccule. These organs inform the brain about changes in the position of the head. When spinning occurs, it causes the vestibular organs to become overstimulated, creating a loss of balance and sometimes nausea.)*

Hey, Children, What's That Sound?
(Listening)

Use this activity to help students make some fun discoveries about the information with which sound provides us. Ahead of time, collect eight different objects that can serve as noisemakers. Direct each student to number a sheet of paper from 1 to 8. Then have students place their heads down on their desks and close their eyes. Make a noise, such as shaking a tambourine, crumpling a sheet of paper, or tapping a pencil on a desk. Challenge each student to listen carefully to find out what made the noise. After you make the sound, hide the item and have students raise their heads. Direct each student to write her guess as to what made the sound on her paper. Then have the students place their heads back on their desks and repeat the exercise with the next sound. After all eight sounds have been heard, reveal what made each sound and have each student add up her correct responses. Ask students to describe how not being able to see affected their hearing. Explain that blind people learn to rely heavily on their sense of hearing and can sometimes hear things the rest of us can't.

"Ears" Looking at You, Kid
(Demonstration)

Not only can ears correctly recognize sounds, but they can also tell the direction from which sounds are coming. Test several volunteers' *binaural hearing,* or hearing with both ears, with this activity. Have a student come to the front of the classroom; then blindfold him. Explain to the student that you will be making a sound on either the left side or the right side of his head. Then, with a rattle or some other noisemaker, make a noise on either side of the student's head and ask him to raise his hand to indicate from which side the noise came. Continue several times. Repeat the activity with other volunteers. Ask students how they can know where sound is coming from even when they are blindfolded. Ask them how hearing can tell direction. *(Explain that a sound made at the left side of a person's head reaches the left ear before it reaches the right ear. The sound is also a little bit louder in the ear closest to it. The brain understands and interprets these tiny differences, letting you know where the sound is coming from.)*

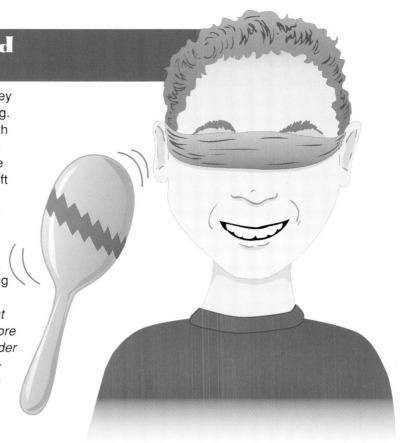

Give Me a Sign
(Introducing Sign Language)

About 15 million people in the United States suffer from hearing loss, and of those, 2 million are deaf. Many hearing-impaired individuals use a system of hand signals known as *sign language* to communicate. Invite someone who knows sign language, such as an interpreter for the deaf, to your class to teach students the signing alphabet or some basic sign language symbols. Afterward, provide each student with a copy of page 45 and have her review the sign language alphabet on that page. Encourage each student to find a partner and together practice the sign language symbols. Then challenge each pair to come up with a short message and practice spelling it out using sign language. Have each pair present its message to the class, challenging the class to interpret the message.

Understanding Hearing Loss
(Experiment, Writing)

Did you know that hearing loss is the most common physical disability in the United States? The number of Americans suffering from a noticeable hearing loss is at least 15 million. Of these people, about 2 million are deaf. However, deafness does not have to be a hindrance to people's success. Many deaf people achieve great things. For example, Ludwig van Beethoven composed some of his most famous music after becoming deaf.

Give your students a greater appreciation for what it's like to have diminished hearing capacity with this activity. Provide each student with a pair of foam earplugs or two cotton balls. Direct the student to wear his earplugs for one day. Lead a class discussion and encourage students to share feelings about their experience. Then have each student write a paragraph describing how his reduced ability to hear affected his day. If desired, extend the activity by having students research famous people who have experienced hearing loss, such as Ronald Reagan (former president), Ludwig van Beethoven (composer), and Curtis Pride (baseball player).

Closed-Captioned Action
(Experiment)

Everybody loves to watch TV. But what would it be like not being able to hear what anyone is saying? Ask students how hearing impairment would affect their viewing habits. Borrow a TV from the media center and have students watch part of a television program with the sound turned off. Ask each student to describe how much of the story she understood with no sound. Ask her to further explain how the lack of sound affected her viewing. Then have the student watch a closed-captioned program with the option on and the sound off. Ask each student to explain how much of the story she understood this time. Point out that closed captioning is designed to allow those who cannot hear, or those with partial hearing, the opportunity to enjoy the same news and entertainment as others.

Give Me a Sign

Directions: Use the symbols on this sheet to practice finger-spelling with sign language.

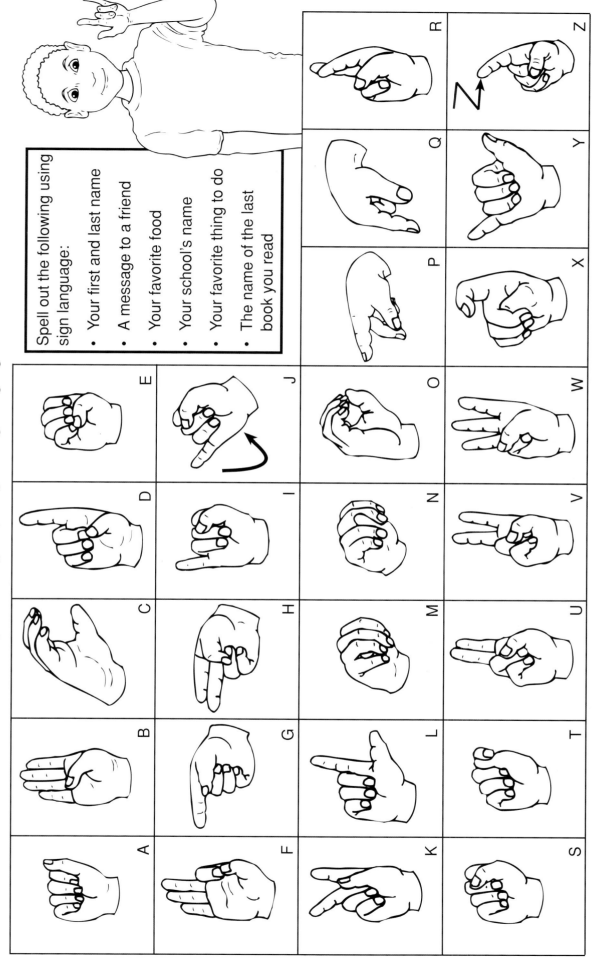

Spell out the following using sign language:

- Your first and last name
- A message to a friend
- Your favorite food
- Your school's name
- Your favorite thing to do
- The name of the last book you read

Note to the teacher: Use with "Give Me a Sign" on page 43.

Let's Hear It for Ears!

Directions: Read each statement below. Decide if it is true or false. If the statement is true, color the ear next to it. Then unscramble the letters on the colored ears to answer the riddle at the bottom of the page.

S   1.   The cochlea is a part of the inner ear that looks like a spiral snail shell.

D   2.   The pinna and the cochlea form the outer ear.

O   3.   The outer ear collects sound waves.

N   4.   The ear is made up of three main sections: the outer ear, the middle ear, and the inner ear.

M   5.   The eardrum separates the outer ear from the inner ear.

H   6.   The three bones of the inner ear are called the handle, the horn, and the saddle.

I   7.   The sound vibrations from the eardrum travel through the bones of the middle ear.

U   8.   Fluid sent to the brain from the inner ear is interpreted as sound.

K   9.   Motion sickness is caused by understimulation of the vestibular organs.

A   10.   Sign language is a communication system of foot gestures and symbols used by the deaf and hearing impaired.

E   11.   Decibels are the units of measurement used to measure sound intensity.

R   12.   People who are not hearing impaired use Morse code to communicate with those who are.

What has nothing left but a nose when it loses an eye?

___ ___ ___ ___ ___

Bonus Box: On the back of this sheet, rewrite each false statement so that it is true.

Name _____

Gettin' Down With Sound

Randy Rocker's ears have heard their share of sounds over the years! Label each part of Randy Rocker's ear with the correct letter. Then number the steps to show the path that the rock 'n' roll sound waves must travel in order for Randy to hear them.

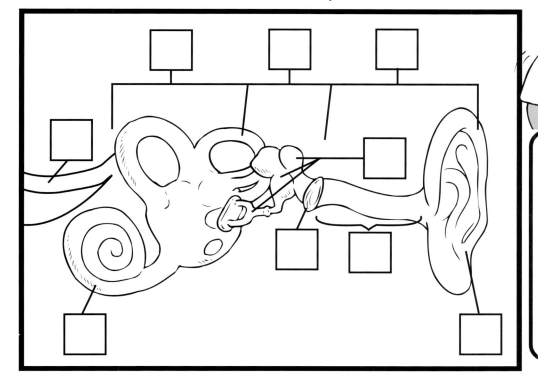

A Ear Canal
B Middle Ear
C Cochlea
D Hammer, Anvil, and Stirrup
E Inner Ear
F Outer Ear
G Nerve Leading to Brain
H Pinna
I Eardrum

_____ Sound waves travel down the ear canal until they reach the eardrum.

_____ Randy's brain decodes the messages from the nerve and he hears the sound.

_____ The vibrations move tiny hairs connected to nerve cells that send impulses to the nerve leading to Randy's brain.

_____ Randy's pinna collects sound waves and acts as a funnel to move them into the ear canal.

_____ The vibrations produced by the eardrum move through the small bones of Randy's middle ear—the hammer, anvil, and stirrup.

_____ The vibrations then move through the fluid that fills the cochlea, a shell-shaped organ in Randy's inner ear.

_____ The sound waves make Randy's eardrum vibrate (move quickly back and forth).

Answer Keys

Page 11
Patti is looking at the cat. The two angles each measure 15°.
Anna is looking at the apple. The two angles each measure 45°.
Emily is looking at the dog. The two angles each measure 75°.
Larry is looking at the cake. The two angles each measure 30°.
Nathan is looking at the banana. The two angles each measure 60°.
Another name for a flat mirror is P L A N E.

Bonus Box answer: Students' drawings will vary, but the angles at which they are drawn should each equal 80°.

Page 12
1. Draw a smiley face at the top of this paper.
2. Write your first, middle, and last names in the bottom left corner.
3. Draw a sun in the upper right corner.
4. Write a sentence using the word "reflection" on the back of this page.
5. Which travels faster, light or sound? Write the answer five times in the lower right corner.
6. List your three favorite foods on the other side.
7. Copy the statement "The angle of incidence equals the angle of reflection" anywhere on this paper.
8. Write the name of an object that is good at reflecting light in the upper left corner.

Page 20
Part One
Station 1: The pencil and ruler appear to be broken or bent.
Station 2: The prism separates rays of light into a rainbow, or spectrum, of colors.
Station 3: The writing on the paper looks magnified.
Station 4: The letters on the paper look magnified.
Station 5: Students will see that they were unable to align the second tube with the first. The tubes will not be in a straight line; it will be a little "off."
Station 6: The line and fish shape covered by the dish appear to be positioned slightly higher on the paper than the line and fish shape not covered by the dish.

Part Two
Students' answers should mention that refracted light is light that bends. Two materials that are good at refracting light are glass and water.

Bonus Box answer: Students' answers will vary.

Page 21
The penny disappears from view.
When water is added to the container, the light from the coin is bent (refracted) upward and goes out of the top of the cup. Because the light does not go out of the side of the cup, the penny is invisible when you look through the side of the cup.

The penny becomes visible.
When water is added to the container, the light is bent down (refracted), making the penny visible through the side of the pie pan.

Page 38
140 threshold of pain, jet takeoff at close range	80 vacuum cleaner
120 amplified rock concert	70 telephone ring
100 circular saw	60 conversation
90 heavy traffic	20 whisper
	0 threshold of audibility

Bonus Box answer: Answers will vary. Accept all reasonable responses.

Page 39
1. human; bat and dolphin
2. dolphin
3. dog
4. 108,985 hertz
5. 132 hertz
6. dolphin, bat, grasshopper, robin

Bonus Box answer: dolphin, bat, grasshopper, robin, human, cat, dog

Page 46
1.	True	7.	True
2.	False	8.	False
3.	True	9.	False
4.	True	10.	False
5.	False	11.	True
6.	False	12.	False

Riddle answer: Noise

Bonus Box answer: Students' answers may vary. Accept reasonable responses.
2. The auricle and the external auditory canal form the outer ear.
5. The eardrum separates the outer ear from the middle ear.
6. The three bones of the middle ear are called the hammer, the anvil, and the stirrup.
8. Nerve impulses sent to the brain from the inner ear are interpreted as sounds.
9. Motion sickness is caused by overstimulation of the vestibular organs.
10. Sign language is a communication system of gestures and hand symbols.
12. People who are not hearing impaired use sign language to communicate with those who are.

Page 47
A Ear Canal
B Middle Ear
C Cochlea
D Hammer, Anvil, and Stirrup
E Inner Ear
F Outer Ear
G Nerve Leading to Brain
H Pinna
I Eardrum

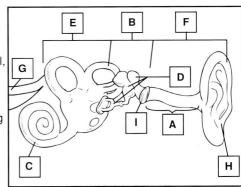

_2_ Sound waves travel down the ear canal until they reach the eardrum.
_7_ Randy's brain decodes the messages from the nerve and he hears the sound.
_6_ The vibrations move tiny hairs connected to nerve cells that send impulses to the nerve leading to Randy's brain.
_1_ Randy's pinna collects sound waves and acts as a funnel to move them into the ear canal.
_4_ The vibrations produced by the eardrum move through the small bones of Randy's middle ear—the hammer, anvil, and stirrup.
_5_ The vibrations then move through the fluid that fills the cochlea, a shell-shaped organ in Randy's inner ear.
_3_ The sound waves make Randy's eardrum vibrate (move quickly back and forth).